TORN
BETWEEN
RELIGION
AND
RELATIONSHIP

A STORY OF HOPE
IN THE MIDST OF
DOMESTIC VIOLENCE

A MEMOIR
JANICE BUTLER

TROY, OHIO

Scripture quotations marked (ESV) are from The Holy Bible, English Standard Version® (ESV®), copyright © 2001 by Crossway, a publishing ministry of Good News Publishers. Used by permission. All rights reserved.

Scripture quotations marked (NIV) are taken from the Holy Bible, New International Version® (NIV®). Copyright © 1973, 1978, 1984 by Biblica, Inc. ™ Used by permission of Zondervan. All rights reserved worldwide.

Requests for information, copyright permissions, or comments should be addressed to:
Clay Bridges Communications & Publishing,
300 South Ridge Avenue, Troy, Ohio, 45373
or info@claybridges.com.

Torn Between Religion and Relationship is a Clay Bridges Communications & Publishing publication. Clay Bridges seeks to provide resources and education to build up people to span life's circumstances. For speaking, training, or author visits, please consult www.claybridges.com or contact us at the information listed above.

Library of Congress Control Number: 2010920584
ISBN: 978-09819807-4-4

Printed and Manufactured in the United States of America

TABLE OF CONTENTS

PART ONE

My Roots: Fearfully and Wonderfully Made

PART TWO

My Journey: The Things We Do For Love

PART THREE

My Reflections: Own Your Stuff; That's How You Grow

SPECIAL THANKS

I first have to say "PRAISE THE LORD!" His praise shall ALWAYS be in my mouth. This book has been challenging. The challenge hasn't been the telling of the story (because it's my personal experience), but it is the overcoming of the obstacles that were trying to keep me from sharing my experience on a larger scale in an effort to help and encourage ladies who are affected by "domestic violence."

I have to say "Thank you" to my family: especially to my mother, Faye Jackson (who is now with the Lord), and to my twin brother, John "Uncle John" Jackson. You guys continually pressed, pushed, and encouraged me to finish the book. You saw the vision before I did, and how my personal testimony would help others. John, I can hear your words so clearly, "Janice, if a woman dies or is hurt because you aren't obedient to God [in sharing your story], then their blood is on you." Although you only said it once, that statement kept playing over and over in my mind. I had to be obedient! Thank you again for all your love, support, and encouragement—pushing me outside of my comfort zone.

Thank you Pastors Eric and Winifred (Winnie) Ashby for prayers, support, and your love. Thank you for pushing me when I didn't think anyone wanted to hear about my experience. You have taught me the "true" meaning of love.

To the "Women of Warfare"... thanks for challenging me in my relationship with God.

A special thanks to Shanel, Lindrea, and Rachel for all the time and effort you put into helping me get this book off the ground. Although I wasn't always sure which direction the book was going to go, please know that I appreciate all your hard work.

DEDICATION

This book is dedicated to: all the women who will read my story and relate to it in some way—even if they've never experienced such a thing—and who will trust God even more as a result. My prayer is that all who read my story would come to know God and understand God has not forgotten them. I pray those women will make a decision and choose to obey the Word of God and never have to walk in my shoes.

Most importantly, this book is dedicated to my family, who has been with me through every step of this journey.

"For I know the plans I have for you," declares the Lord, "plans to prosper you and not to harm you, plans to give you hope and a future" (Jeremiah 29:11, NIV).

PROLOGUE

Whenever I tell this story, I get looks of disbelief. But as difficult as it might be to believe, it is true. I share it with everyone who will listen, especially young women, who are beginning the journey of "Life" filled with promise, expectation, hope, and the dream for happily-ever-after, but are not sure where to go or how to get there.

This book is more than just a story; for me it was truly a journey. It was a journey of learning—learning God's place in my life and my place in His plan. Through the journey, my relationship with God became the most important relationship in my life. Without that relationship as a foundation, nothing else in my life could help me stand up to the trials I faced. I would not wish on anyone the experiences I lived through on my journey. They were hard lessons to learn, but through them I learned what God's purposes are for my life.

I believe one of my life purposes, and a reason why I am alive today, is to share my story with other women who can listen and learn from my mistakes without having to experience their own painful lessons. If you are in an unhealthy relationship, I hope you pay attention to the experiences I went through and learn to recognize the signs of an abusive relationship.

THE JOURNEY

Because of the head trauma, I felt like I was going to pass out. Robert, my husband, walked me around the house so I stayed awake. He put ice on my wound.

He was getting really nervous. He decided we needed to get out of the house and go some place where no one could find us. But when he opened the door, the police put the spotlight on us. He grabbed me and put me in front of him like a human shield. He realized that they had the place surrounded.

He quickly closed the door. We were alone again in the chaos. We could hear the S.W.A.T. team on the roof and in the front yard. We could see the infrared beams through the windows. Robert was trying to find a safe place in the house away from the windows and the police. He was shoving me from place to place. He was getting more and more nervous.

He had to think. He was asking himself, "What have I done?" He was feeling trapped. There was no way out.

He thought he had a good plan. It should have been quick. Nobody would have known until it was too late. But it didn't play out that way.

Robert's behavior was erratic. One minute he was calm and seemingly rational, the next minute he was angry and volatile.

As I faced the horror of my situation and my death, I reflected on my dreams of what my life should have been…my dreams were nowhere near my reality. *So much for childhood dreams…*

PART ONE
MY ROOTS

FEARFULLY AND WONDERFULLY MADE

While growing up, I dreamed the dream of a little girl: of marriage and a happy life with a husband and children. I dreamed of a husband who would love and respect me; I dreamed of being a loving wife and mother. But, I also dreamed my marriage would be different from (and better than) my parent's marriage.

Like my dad, my husband would provide for us by working, paying bills, and making sure we didn't want for anything. Unlike my dad, my husband wouldn't go party every weekend without his wife, drinking and seeing other women. I dreamed of a husband who would treat me like a queen. I dreamed our love would stand strong and withstand the inevitable storms of life.

Like I said, "I dreamed..."

MY CHILDHOOD

Parental relationships

I grew up in what I thought was a very loving family. My mother and father were both in the home. My father was the breadwinner, but my mother worked hard, too. My parents loved each other and raised my older brother Michael, my twin brother John, and me to love each other. My father always kissed my mother and told her, "I love you" when he left for work.

We went on family vacations, visited our relatives every Sunday for dinner, and had family gatherings. We seemed to be a "normal" family.

Familial relationships

Even though both of my parents were in the home, my mother really raised us. She is the one who instilled morals in us. She taught us to be honest with people and to love and care for others.

My mother was the "community" mom. She was the mother at all the games—volleyball, basketball, football, baseball, and track meets. She was my support and my cheerleader, the glue that held us all together. From her I learned that no matter what goes on inside the house, you hold it together.

My father was an over-the-road truck driver and was gone several days a week. When Friday came, he went out partying. Sometimes he carried his partying on throughout the weekend and would not come home until Sunday. He was a good provider, though. Even though he partied, he took care of our family. We didn't want for anything, except more time with him. Michael was eight years older than John and me. He went to the local public school, while John and I went to a Catholic school, which was rare for the black children in our neighborhood.

I know my father loved me—I was "Daddy's Little Girl." But I didn't realize how important it is for a girl to "see" and "know" her daddy's love. When I look back, my dad didn't show a lot of outward expressions of love towards me, except to respond when I told him, "I love you" as he left for work or to go out. He didn't reach out to hug or hold me. He never really told me he loved me until I got older. But when my father was home, we watched TV together, and he took me with him on out-of-town trips to see his family in Louisiana. I seemed to get my way with him. If I asked for something, he always got it for me. Yet there was still something missing.

It is interesting what you remember about your childhood when you are trying to sort out the past. I remember wanting to sit on my dad's lap when I was about twelve or thirteen-years-old. My dad was at home, which was rare during the week, and we were watching TV. I tried to sit on his lap, and he pushed me off and said, "Girl, you can't do that. Get off my lap." I was hurt and confused because I didn't know why he pushed me off his lap. I thought, "I am your little girl, what's wrong with me sitting on your lap?" I started feeling there was something wrong with me, and my dad didn't really love me.

I did not realize how much that affected me until much later in life. It wasn't until I was an adult and was talking to my mother about all the things I'd been through that she explained why my dad wouldn't let me sit on his lap, and why he didn't show much affection. She explained that he was not very affectionate, and it had nothing to do with me. My dad had come from a very big family. His mother died after her sixteenth child. My father left home when he was twelve-years-old, and he had to learn on his own what it meant to love and to show love.

I still didn't quite understand how that affected his treatment of me as his daughter. But, as I grew up, I started to realize I missed his validation and sought it in other male figures. That feeling of neglect began a string of empty relationships.

I was looking for the love that only a father could give a daughter. I needed male acceptance because I did not get it from the first male in my life—my dad. I did not understand how that experience affected me until I started searching my own heart—after three marriages. The rejection caused me to think less of myself. It made me think I was not lovable. If my dad could not show me love, what other man could?

Every man I liked was like my father in some way. All the guys I had relationships with—my boyfriends, my husbands—loved to party.

Dating relationships

As I look back to my grade school years, some of the experiences I had with other males also contributed to my self-doubt and my feelings of being different.

At an early age, boys liked me, and I called them my boyfriends. I remember in the third grade, I said I was "going" with this boy, but I wanted to break up with him to go with someone else. The boy told me at lunch he was going to beat me up if I broke up with him. Because, in his own words, "I could not just quit him." Even though I was scared, I didn't tell anyone about his threat. After school, my brother John and I were on our way to catch the city bus when the boy, who was a fourth grader, caught up with us and pushed me down in the snow. He told me I couldn't just decide to break up with him. I just sat there hoping he wouldn't hit me. Then he let me go. By the time we got to the bus stop, we had missed our bus. I was really embarrassed and nervous. While we waited for the next bus, I asked my brother why he didn't defend me. He said, "There was no need for both of us to get beat up."

I still broke up with the boy. I told him he was not going to beat up on me and expect me to remain his girlfriend. The next time I got a boyfriend, I was careful not to make him angry or to do anything that would make him not want to be with me. Notice I said, "Not want to be with me." That is very different than not wanting them to hurt me.

I look at how these early relationships were the beginning of my trying to be something for somebody else and looking for a protector to come to my rescue. I did not realize how much of an effect those "so called" relationships had on my later choice in men.

My mother made it clear that I wouldn't be allowed to date until I became a teenager. But by then some patterns were already being formed.

My mother was strict when it came to boys. After I turned sixteen-years-old and was allowed to go out, I still had to go out in a group or double date with my twin brother. I would call my date and tell him where to meet us. I was seventeen-years-old and going into my senior year when I finally went out with a boy by myself.

My mother talked to me about how my body would change. She told me what to expect when I started developing into a young lady, but she didn't say a lot about sex. The few times she did talk to me about sex, she simply said, "Do not have sex because you will get pregnant."

I heard every word she said, but I didn't plan on getting pregnant, because I wasn't even sexually active. But I constantly dreamed of being married one day.

CHAPTER TWO

MY MARRIAGES BEGIN

I believed that my husband was supposed to be the head of the house and the protector. My husband was supposed to be my confidante and friend. I wanted to be a caring and loving wife, and I wanted a caring and loving husband. I believed that if I did my part, my husband wouldn't need to leave the house for another woman—or so I thought.

I took this attitude into marriage after marriage, expecting a different result with each attempt. But the result was always the same. It was like the description of insanity—repeating the same behavior and expecting different results. I kept asking the question, "What am I not doing or doing too much of?"

But, I still wanted that happily-ever-after dream more than I wanted to acknowledge my reality. I had been willing to do "whatever it took" to make it come true, even if that meant ignoring major problems and red flags. I had done everything I knew to do, and then some, in an attempt to be happy and have the fairy tale life I wanted. But no matter what I did, things didn't change, and nothing seemed to work for very long. Then I started asking serious questions—questions that make you look inside.

What was wrong with me? Why did all my relationships cause so much hurt and pain? Was it me? What was I doing or not doing? Did I not love him enough? Did I not do enough for him? I didn't understand, and I couldn't find answers to my questions.

My childhood dreams of happily-ever-after haven't yet become reality. I never dreamed I would be married multiple times.

Bryan Enters My Life

I was a junior in high school when I met my first husband. He was a year older than I was and attended a local public high school. I played volleyball, ran track, and was a cheerleader. He played baseball for his school. We were both popular and outgoing. He came to my games and hung out with my friends and me afterward. He had his own car and a little money.

As we spent more time together, he started asking me to have sex with him. I was a virgin, but he was already sexually active. I was very naïve and didn't know what to do. I didn't want him to break up with me to start seeing someone else. And, I was willing to do whatever it took to make him want to stay with me. Little did I know at the time, he was already messing around with other girls from his school.

I wasn't educated about STDs and birth control methods because my mother did not talk to me about it. She just told me not to have sex before I was married, because it wasn't right in God's sight. I didn't want to disappoint or upset my mother, but it was more important to me not to lose my boyfriend.

The summer before my senior year, I eventually gave in to his pressure, because I thought I was in love and was leaving for cheerleading camp in a few weeks. So, before I left, I agreed to have sex one time.

While at cheerleading camp in Oklahoma, I started feeling sick. Our chaperone took me to see the nurse who tested my urine.

She told me that I was pregnant.

I didn't tell any of the girls because I was shocked and worried about telling my parents. The nurse gave me some medicine, and I finished out the week.

When I got back home to Kansas City, I knew that I had to tell everybody that I was pregnant. I had to tell my parents, the girls on the cheerleading squad, my boyfriend, and my Catholic schoolteachers. I had to make decisions on how I was going to finish out the school year.

I ended up meeting with the cheerleaders first during practice, and I told them that I had to quit the squad because I was pregnant. Some of my best friends were shocked and disappointed. I was so embarrassed. I knew I had let them down and my life was about to change.

Next, I had to tell mother and father. I was so scared to tell them because I didn't know what my mother would do to me, and what my father would say. When I finally told my mother I was pregnant, she was so disappointed in me. My father didn't say a word, which made me feel really uncomfortable because I couldn't tell if he was mad, disappointed or experiencing some other emotions and thoughts.

When I broke the news to my boyfriend, I thought he seemed excited. I told my boyfriend, "We've got to get married." I thought that if we got married, my mother wouldn't be so disappointed in me, and then the sex and resulting pregnancy would be made right in the sight of God. Besides, I didn't want to be a single mother. I wanted to be with my child's father.

My whole life changed, but not in the way I wanted.

I was a senior in high school when my son, Daimon was born. I remained in school and graduated seventh in my class in May of 1980. Despite receiving several scholarships, I didn't go to college. Instead, Bryan and I got married that September. The day before the wedding, I kept thinking, "It's not too late to call off the wedding. Don't do it!" But I didn't want the embarrassment of cancelling the day before the wedding. Some of my relatives had come from out of town, and my parents had spent so much money on the wedding and reception. I couldn't back out. What would people say about me? I felt trapped.

On September 13, 1980, I married my son's father, as planned. My new husband wasn't very responsible and could not keep a job. I did everything: paid the bills, took care of our son, and kept the house in order. Sometimes we didn't have anything to eat except potatoes. At those times he would leave Daimon and me at home to go eat at his mother's house. On weekends, Bryan went out gambling and partying, then he came home and expected me to perform my wifely duties.

Although we were legally married for two years, we separated after nine months of marriage. I couldn't take it any longer. I felt like I was alone in the marriage. But I also felt that divorce wasn't the perfect will of God. During our time of separation, I kept trying to make it work. Sometimes Bryan acted like he really wanted a family, and other times he seemed not to care. I finally realized that he would come around and tell me what I wanted to hear when it was "convenient." But when he was doing his own thing, he stayed away. Bryan picked arguments and blamed me because our marriage wasn't working. Although he was cheating on me with other women, I felt I had to stay committed to him because I had made a vow "for better or worse." And if he thought I was seeing someone else, he'd start accusing me of breaking up our family.

After being separated for nearly a year-and-a-half, I was visiting my girlfriend when he came by to talk to me. I was uneasy and told my girlfriend to watch out the window while I went outside. He started yelling at me about seeing someone else. I tried to walk away, but he grabbed me and pushed me to the ground. He hit me in the face, giving me a black eye. That was it. Between the cheating, lies, and now physical attacks, I had finally had enough. I had tried to keep the peace because we had a son together, but I wasn't going to get hurt either.

Michael Enters My Life

While I was separated from Bryan, I met my second husband, Michael. He was playing in a band with a friend of mine at the National Guard Armory. During the band's break, I asked my friend to introduce me to him. He was the lead singer and bass guitar player for the group. After our introduction, we were immediately attracted to each other. When he got back on stage, it was as if he was singing to me. I felt like I was falling in love with him.

When we first started seeing each other, he was seeing someone else, so we had to sneak around. I was only thinking about what I wanted, and how he made me feel. I wasn't even considering his girlfriend's feelings. It was all about me, and yes, it was out of character for me, but I decided, "Why should I always be the 'good' girl?" No one seemed to care about what I wanted, and if I didn't go after what I wanted, then I'd never get it. He and his girlfriend eventually broke up, so we didn't need to sneak around anymore, and we started openly dating in 1982.

Michael had a beautiful voice and I imagined that he would be famous someday. I wanted to feel that I was a part of his dream. I was going to be the woman behind the man. We would have the dream I always wanted. I knew I didn't want to be just his girlfriend. I wanted the title "wife." I already had a son, and I didn't want to be someone he just had sex with and didn't intend to marry. I didn't want to be one of those girls. I wanted a committed relationship. I knew my mother wouldn't approve of my having sex out of wedlock, and I didn't want her to be disappointed in me again. I also knew that God wasn't pleased with me either. I was trying to live according to the Bible, but apparently I wanted this man more than I wanted a pleasing relationship with God. The struggle within me started again.

In my mind, we had to get married. I wasn't going to be taken advantage of again. This time I would take control. He wasn't going to keep coming over for four or five days at a time to stay at my house just to have sex with me and then go home. I wanted to know that he loved me, and told him that we needed to marry or break up and just be friends.

I don't think the pressure mattered to him. He wanted a place of his own, and we were already playing house, "So why not get married?" he must have thought. We got married in June, 1983. We had a small wedding at his uncle's house. It wasn't the wedding I wanted, but I pretended it didn't matter because I'd already had a big wedding. It was only a ceremony. We didn't have a lot of money, so we didn't go on a honeymoon. But Michael had a singing gig that evening, so we celebrated at the club. He sang a tribute to me that made me feel special.

We were married for about six months before I got pregnant. I was expecting a little girl. Michael was very sensitive to my needs and made sure I was comfortable. He was so attentive, and I was really happy and loved every moment that I was pregnant.

After our daughter Taukia was born, he was working off and on. When he wasn't working, he'd watch her so we could save on babysitting fees. But our money was getting tight, and we were trying to live on just my salary. That's when the arguing started.

I started nagging him to get a job so he could help out financially. That was when he started leaving after I got home from work and staying at band practice for long hours. I started wondering if he was cheating on me. Sometimes I would pack my kids in the car and go out to find him when he didn't come home.

One day while I was driving home from work, I saw him on the street talking to a woman. I confronted him when he got home, and we had a huge argument over it. We hardly spoke to each other after that.

I decided that if he could stay out and come home whenever he wanted, I would start going out myself. One night I went out with some girlfriends and didn't come home until around 3:00 A.M. He thought I had been out with a man and accused me of cheating on him. I told him, "Just because you're seeing someone doesn't mean that I'm doing the same thing."

During that argument, he slapped me. I was shocked. He had never hit me before. I told him he had to leave. He packed a few clothes and left without a fuss. I don't know where he went, but I figured he was going to his girlfriend's house.

I saw them out walking one day, and it really bothered me. I wasn't going to let him treat me like that. We had fought, and I had asked him to leave, but I didn't want our marriage to end. He had given up on our marriage and was already moving on with someone else. That was like another slap in the face.

I thought to myself, "You're supposed to love me. I'm your wife. Why aren't you fighting for our marriage? Why is this so easy for you to give up?" Then I began to wonder if this was payback for dating him when he had a girlfriend. As the old saying goes, "What goes around comes around." I thought I was getting what I deserved for taking him away from his old girlfriend.

A few weeks later, he came home and started packing the rest of his things. He told me he didn't want me anymore, and he was through with all the arguing and fighting. He didn't want me to bother him because he'd found someone else. I was devastated. How could he give up after three years of marriage? How could he leave his daughter?

For weeks I tried to figure out where I had gone wrong. I would chase him. I wanted him to explain the problem and tell me what I could do. I would sit outside his girlfriend's house for hours, waiting for him to come outside. Day after day, I thought of new ways to try to get in touch with him. But nothing worked. He avoided me. Finally, I decided that I had no choice but to give in and file for divorce.

Afterward, I became depressed. I started drinking hard liquor in an attempt to numb the pain. I even became suicidal. I couldn't understand why my two husbands had cheated on me and then left me. I tried to be everything for them. But it became clearer and clearer to me that I was a torn and damaged person. I had no clue where or when the damage started. My past failed relationships haunted me. The pain was fresh, and the memories were vivid. Why couldn't my husbands love me like I loved them?

But here I was, in my mid-twenties and already divorced twice with two children: a son, Daimon, from my first marriage and a daughter, Taukia, from my second marriage. I did everything for my husbands and boyfriends because I thought that was love. I would buy things for them, and I was always available to do whatever and go wherever they wanted to go. I thought that was what you did to get and keep a man. I tried in my own strength to make the relationships work, but they always failed.

Because that is not what true love is about.

And unfortunately, it seems I had not learned my lesson yet.

PART ONE

APPLICATIONS FROM THE AUTHOR

Healthy Early Relationship Habits

I believe it's important to start talking to your daughters early. Don't be ashamed or afraid to discuss sexual topics with them. They are getting exposed to different situations at school or when they are hanging out. You'd be surprised at what our young girls are dealing with and talking about. We have to be honest with our daughters about what a healthy relationship looks like. Talk to her about the signs of abuse (verbal, mental, and physical) and unhealthy relationships and how they evolve.

I also believe parents should teach their sons to respect girls, that a real man wants to protect a young girl from being hurt – not be the one hurting or using girls to gain acceptance from their peers. Parents should remind their sons that each girl is somebody's sister or daughter, and an abused woman could be his sister, mother, aunt, or cousin. Ask how he would feel if one of his female relatives was being abused? It is also not okay for girls/women to abuse boys/men. Unfortunately, that is happening more these days as well. So parents should talk to their sons about the signs of abuse and unhealthy relationships also.

Wisdom for Dating

Prayer and obedience are the keys to finding your mate. You have to know who you are and be confident in yourself if you want the respect and love of others. Learn what your strengths and weaknesses, likes and dislikes, are before you get involved with someone. Define the standards you intend to live by, which should be from the Word of God. Know what you will and will not take, and don't settle for anything less than that. We teach people how to treat us by behaviors we allow. If we don't already have specific boundaries set, men will take advantage of us. Don't let a man's flattering words get you off track or pull you in.

You won't be desperate for a relationship if you know that the man is getting a prize! Proverbs 18:22 (ESV) says, "He who finds a wife, finds a good thing and obtains favor from the Lord."

Reflections: The Proverbs 31 Woman

I wrote this for those feeling alone. I am fearfully and wonderfully made, as are you. I am not alone, you are not alone.

When I study the scripture and read Proverbs 31, I see the many characteristics and traits she possessed. As I began to grow and accept my worth, I began to desire those same characteristics. I've come to believe that I can be a Proverbs 31 woman, and a godly man will appreciate that kind of woman. If I hadn't learned this lesson, I believe the cycle of tragedy would have continued in my life and in the lives of my children. I did not want that for my daughter or my son.

It is a lonely place—being married and feeling like you are alone. If you are in that place, you can avoid loneliness with wise counsel from those who have gone ahead of you.

It took time for me to believe I was fearfully and wonderfully made. We can all pass by a mirror and think, "I need to lose weight," or "I need to get a nose job," or any other self-depreciating thought. That is self-loathing, not self-love.

Each day I try to find something positive about myself and focus on it. Think what would happen if I could walk past that same mirror and say, "I like what God created. I am fearfully and wonderfully made."

PART TWO

MY JOURNEY

My first two marriages did not go as planned. They did not see what a jewel I was and did not appreciate me. The next one, I thought to myself, he'll see my worth. I'll work extra hard.

For each relationship, I was willing to put in overtime. I was willing to be more understanding, and I told myself I just needed more patience. I came to the conclusion that having more patience would not be a problem. In the back of my mind, I knew the Word said in 2 Corinthians 6:14, "Do not be unequally yoked with unbelievers." But I told myself over and over, "Surely God will understand. I have to make the next relationship work. Because I know it's God's will for me to be married." I read in the Word that the unbelieving husband is "sanctified by his wife." So I rationalized that because I had accepted Jesus as my Savior and am now saved that my husband will also be saved. But giving up on my dream was not an option. I was torn between religion and wanting a fulfilling relationship. According to the Word of God, the Lord said he would give me the desires of my heart. And my heart's desire was to be married – "happily ever after." So in 1990 my journey began with the man who changed my life forever.

CHAPTER THREE

MY JOURNEY WITH ROBERT BEGINS

Robert and I met at a barbeque through a mutual friend. I was attracted to him instantly—to his rugged good looks and suave demeanor. When he walked into the room, I couldn't take my eyes off him. He had a smooth way about him. It made me take notice. Boy, he was fine!

I happened to be cooking the meat on the grill that day. As I walked out to the backyard, I noticed that he was noticing me. I stayed outside longer than I needed to just to see if he'd come outside. And sure enough, he eventually walked outside and asked if I needed any help. He made a joke about how I probably didn't know what I was doing and could use his assistance. Of course, I just laughed and played along. We talked awhile and sort of forgot about the food cooking. I believe he was sizing me up while at the same time, I was checking him out, too.

He didn't stay around at the barbeque long. When he left, I asked my girlfriend to give me the "411" on him. I was mostly interested in whether he was dating anyone. She said he was not dating anyone in particular, but that they were close friends. Although she was separated from her husband, she was still married, so I knew nothing should happen between them.

A few weeks later, my girlfriend and I were hanging out, and I was really depressed. I hadn't been out on a date in a while, and I just wanted some companionship, so I asked her if she thought Robert would be interested in going to the movies. She called and asked him for me. He agreed. My friend gave Robert my phone number, we talked on the phone and set a date.

That Saturday we went to the movie and then out to eat. We talked for hours. It was a really good first date. After a few phone conversations and meeting with each other for lunch, we made it official and started dating in August, 1990.

Even though I was attending church and knew what the scripture said, I didn't apply the Word to my daily life. My focus was only on what I wanted. And I wanted to be married. I wanted so much to be in a committed relationship as a wife that my desires overshadowed my relationship with God. It didn't matter to me that Robert wasn't saved. Because I was saved. I thought my salvation was enough for both of us. I always knew I was supposed to be with a Christian man. But, I thought I could change him and that he would accept Christ into his heart if he just stuck with me. I liked this guy so I thought I could make it work, but that is not how God intended it to be. My thinking and my strong desire to be married at any cost was contrary to what the Word of God said, "Be not unequally yoked with unbelievers" (2 Corinthians 6:14).

As I said earlier, Robert was a nice-looking, turn-your-head-twice kind of guy. He seemed to have himself together. He had a good job working for the railroad, had his own car and his own apartment. We did a lot of things together in the beginning. We went to the movies; hung out together with his three sons and my two children, who got along well together. He had family and friends over to play cards and to sit around listening to music. We were like a family when we all got together. When he went out to the clubs or to a friend's party, I went along with him because I was going to be the woman behind the man and support him in everything he did.

I thought he was different from my last two husbands. He seemed to enjoy my being around him. We had so much fun. It seemed so right that we were a couple. I was his girlfriend, not just someone he hung out with. I felt like he treated me differently than my ex-husbands did because it seemed like he wanted me and wasn't just tolerating me. He would call me just to ask me how my day was. I didn't feel like I was chasing him, so for me that was a step in the right relationship direction. So I figured it didn't matter if he partied and drank—who doesn't have an area they needed to work on? He'd change.

The more time we spent together, the more Robert told me about his past. He revealed that he had been in jail before. But I appreciated that he was honest with me up front. He told me that he had a criminal record for holding his youngest son's family hostage. He even showed me the newspaper article about it and explained that he was in love with his son's mother and couldn't think about them not being together. So, while in a drunken stupor, he decided that if he couldn't be with her then he didn't want to live.

I was a little taken aback because I'd never been with someone that had committed such a serious crime. But I rationalized, "Oh, he is reformed. He has done his time. He deserves a chance. Everybody should get the benefit of the doubt." Mentally, I went back and forth finally justifying his actions and what he'd done, and making it okay in my mind that it's okay to have a relationship with him. Because surely, he wouldn't do anything like that again. He doesn't want to go back to jail or get killed. He took responsibility for his actions and has learned from them, so I thought. Plus, he was all of the things my first two husbands were not—he had his own stuff and wasn't expecting me to take care of him.

While we dated, other women always tried to get with him. I was always finding phone numbers in his pants or around his house, but I convinced myself that it didn't matter because he was with me. He partied every weekend, but he was with me. So I accepted that partying and going out on the weekends is what he did. That was Robert's way of having fun. I got used to other women calling and to the fact that other women were interested in him. And although I knew about the other women and the phone numbers, I was trying so hard to keep him that I never addressed the problem.

I saw the signs but chose to ignore them. A couple of times, Robert broke up with me to be with somebody else.

I remember one particular lady Robert met at a club. I never met her, but I knew she lived in Columbia, Missouri, which is about two hours from Kansas City, where we lived. He went to visit her, and she came see him regularly. I just sat back and waited. During the week, I was number one in his life. But on the weekend he told me, "I am having company." I knew what that meant. Time and time again, I tried to convince myself that the other relationships wouldn't last long. I told myself that I was glad he was honest and not cheating on me behind my back. But what was worse: knowing that he was seeing other people while waiting for him to come back. or being a fool for putting up with his mess?

Nevertheless, I just waited. I did not want to fail at another relationship. I actually thought it was my fault. I believed his behavior was because of something I had or had not done. "Why didn't this thing work?" I thought. It was not even about me anymore. He was doing his own thing. But, instead of just letting go and moving on, I waited until he got tired of the other woman. I wanted him to see I was a good and patient woman. I just knew he'd come back.

After five years of dating off and on, Robert finally told me he was ready to settle down. I felt that all the waiting and torment I had gone through finally paid off.

CHAPTER FOUR

MY JOURNEY WITH ROBERT DEEPENS

In March of 1995, Robert asked me to marry him. I was at his apartment one afternoon, and we were having lunch. He asked me to take a ride with him, so we got in the car and went to a pawn shop not far from his place. He knew that I liked to look at rings, so he asked me to pick out some rings that I liked. We frequently went to pawn shops to look for stuff, so it wasn't anything unusual because I realized that you could find really good diamonds there for a lot less than you would pay at a jewelry store. I picked out a ring that I really liked, and he asked me if I wanted to buy it. I just laughed and asked what's going on. He told me that he had been doing a lot of thinking and that he wanted to marry me. At first, I thought he was playing, but he bought the ring right then. I was nervous and excited at the same time. Later that weekend, we went over to his sister's house where some of his family was, and he announced that he had proposed.

After Robert proposed, the thought of getting married was beginning to sink in, and my mind was telling me that this is what I had been asking for, but my heart and soul were having some serious doubts.

I thought about all the other women and wondered, what happened? What's different and what made him decide to settle down? I thought I would be happy, but something inside of me just didn't feel right. I didn't know what it was. I was supposed to be happy because I had waited five years for this man to ask me to marry him. I looked at all I had to go through just to get to this point, but I was nervous and uneasy inside. So I prayed, "Oh, Lord, help me! Show me what to do because I do not want to make another mistake. Is this the man you have for me?"

God's Warning

Although I had been in a relationship with Robert, off and on for nearly five years, one good thing was that I was growing as a Christian during that time. I was beginning to know Christ and to hear from God with the ability to recognize His voice. I was getting into the Word and believing the Bible. I was studying and praying. One day while I was in prayer, the Holy Spirit spoke to me and said:

"This is not who I have for you, but if you choose to marry him, you are going to have to do three things:
- Trust Me totally. Stop listening to others and depend totally on Me.
- Get into the Word daily so you will know and hear the voice of God.
- Read I Corinthians 7:10-16."

The Lord said if I would do these three things He would "keep me." I didn't exactly know what he meant by "keep me," but it didn't really matter. The three things that the Lord told me to do seemed so easy. I said, "Wow, I can do that!"

When I read the scripture He had given me in first Corinthians, it seemed to confirm my thoughts that Robert is going to accept Christ into his life and be saved. I really held on to the part of scripture that stated, "….the unbelieving husband is sanctified by the wife." That was all I needed to see. I started thinking, "He is going to get saved because I am saved." God is going to bless me so I just knew the Lord was going to work my relationship with Robert out. But, that is not what God said. He said He would keep me. So, I followed the instructions that the Lord gave

34

me. I got into the Word and read the scriptures every day. I was learning to trust God for the things I needed. I wasn't feeling nervous anymore about marrying Robert. I learned to hear the Lord's voice and how He spoke to me even though I knew my choice was not God's perfect plan for my life.

But I believe that the Lord knew I would choose to marry Robert, in spite of His warning.

Our Marriage

Robert and I planned to get married in May of 1995, and I started planning for the wedding. I made my own invitations and mailed them out. We weren't going to have a big wedding because we wanted to save as much money as we could in case we decided to go on a honeymoon later. Since Robert lived in an apartment and I already had a house, we agreed that it didn't make sense for him to pay rent for two months, so he turned in his notice at his apartment and moved in with me. I really didn't feel bad about living together, because in a couple months we would be husband and wife. But, two weeks before the wedding, Robert decided he wasn't ready to get married. He said he wasn't sure if he was really ready to settle down. He admitted that he was getting nervous because marriage is a big commitment, and he didn't take that commitment or the vows lightly. Although I was hurt, confused, and disappointed, I admired the fact that he told me about his feelings before we got married. I really respected that in him, and I didn't want to get married again and have it end in divorce.

But after he called off the wedding, we continued living together. The Holy Spirit convicted me so bad about it that I couldn't sleep some nights. I knew I was going against the will of God by living with Robert and having sex with someone I wasn't married to. I also felt bad because I wasn't being a good example for my children of how a Christian woman should carry herself and deal with relationships. I was being a hypocrite by telling my kids to do what the Word says, but yet I wasn't. I didn't want them to grow up and think that they didn't have to be committed in a relationship. Or that instead of asking God to send them the mate He has for them, that they should shop around and try to find the "right" person themselves.

Finally, about the middle of June, I said to Robert, "Look, you cannot stay here any more. I can't do this. The Holy Spirit is whipping my tail about our living together." I was struggling with doing what the Word says and having my own desires met. Robert didn't put up a fuss when I asked him to leave. He said he understood and respected my feelings. He also understood that I had children and that I didn't want my children to get the idea that people should live together just to satisfy their needs.

I really believed that Robert understood where I was coming from and respected my position as a Christian, although it didn't matter to him. So he moved back to his old apartment complex, and our relationship didn't seem to really change. Actually, things seemed to get better. I thought we had a better understanding and respect for each other. I respected the fact that he was able to tell me before we got married, and I believe he respected me for standing up to him when I was uncomfortable about our living arrangements. He knew I was serious about my relationship with God, and he respected that.

When Robert moved out, I got some relief spiritually. I wasn't feeling as guilty. When we were engaged, I told myself that it was okay to have sex because we were about to get married. But now that we weren't planning on getting married, I couldn't use that excuse or rationale for having sex. I knew I did the right thing by asking him to move out.

About a month later, Robert and I were talking, and he said he realized that I was always going to be there for him. He knew I was the one for him. Even as I listened to him and thought back to the times when he saw other women while we were together, the weekends he did not come home, the times he just didn't seem to appreciate me, and even the fact that he called off the wedding once, the hard part seemed to be over with him. So when he said he realized I was always going to be there for him, it really validated me and made me feel like all of my hard work, long suffering, and patience finally paid off—again.

Robert and I told all of our children that although we had called off the wedding a few months ago, we decided to get married in July. They didn't really seem too phased by the announcement because they were used to us being together and, sadly enough, not being together.

We got married in July of 1995 at the courthouse.

My family was not there, but one of his sisters and brother-in-law came as witnesses. It was a simple ceremony. I always wondered what it was like to be married by a justice-of-the-peace. We had to wait in line because there were other couples at the courthouse getting married. So when they called our names, we went into a conference room and stood in front of a man that we had met just then and exchanged vows. It took all of ten to fifteen minutes, but it was legal, and we'd finally done it. We had finally committed our lives to one another.

We were married for four months before everything changed: not for better, but for worse.

CHAPTER FIVE

OUR JOURNEY ON THE FIRST HILL

During that time, Robert started staying out more on the weekends and drinking more during the week, but I didn't notice any drastic changes in our relationship. There were a lot of things going on.

Worldly Pressures

Robert had decided to quit his job at the local newspaper and become a mechanic full time. Working on cars is what he loved to do. and he was a good mechanic. Although our household income went down, I supported his decision. The problem was that he got stressed about not having any money.

At the same time, he was served with papers from the Family Court for child support for all three of his sons. And. of course, the courts were taking both our incomes into consideration, which meant more money going out and not enough coming in. So he drank more. Drinking is what seemed to help him forget about the immediate pressures or issues that he was facing.

Every Friday evening at five (like clockwork) he started drinking beer. Fridays meant he went to the club, or we had company over to play cards or dominoes while hanging out. There was always beer, liquor, and weed. There were times when Robert went out and did not come home until the next day. His excuse was that he took some friend (meaning a woman) home, and then, because he was too drunk to drive, he just slept on the couch or that he stayed at his sister's for safety reasons. I didn't believe him, but what was I supposed to do?

I dreaded the weekends. I never knew if he was coming home. But I knew that Robert was like this before we got married, so I couldn't expect him to change just because we got married.

Now don't get me wrong or think everything was bad. We did have some really good times. It was fun having family and friends over. It was nice when Robert and I rented a movie and just sat around and cuddled. Sometimes we got up in the middle of the night, woke the kids up, and went to Shoney's for the breakfast buffet.

Robert loved to go fishing on the weekends. Sometimes we went as a family, and other times, he called me from the lake to ask me to come out and sit with him. I fix sandwiches or picked up something to eat for a picnic while he fished.

I took food down to the repair shop, where he worked, and I believe it made Robert feel good. He loved it and bragged about what a good woman I was to him in front of his buddies. So everything wasn't bad and it was the good times that I held onto. They gave me hope in handling the rough, rocky times as we began to slip down the slope.

Weeks and months went by where the bad times started outweighing the good. I started feeling neglected because he wasn't spending time with me, but whenever he came home, he expected me to perform my wifely duties. I began to feel used and angry.

We seemed to argue all the time about little things. I couldn't do anything right in his eyes, and everything seemed to be my fault. Emotionally, I was getting worn out and tired.

I started to notice that whenever I came home from work, I had anxiety or panic attacks as I approached the house and saw his car in the driveway. I just didn't know what kind of mood Robert was going to be in. I was nervous and didn't want to upset him, but at the same time, I didn't hold my tongue either.

I wanted us to communicate and talk things out, but he never felt like talking. It was so frustrating because I wanted to help. I don't know what I could have done, but I was willing to try anything.

Despite all of the drama, I always felt that loving Robert meant putting up with a lot of stuff. I felt that because we were married, I had to accept whatever he put out. According to the scripture the man is the "head" and the wife is to be submissive to her husband. Wasn't that what a good wife is supposed to do? I accepted that he was not the perfect man when we got married, but I could not and would not turn back. I made a vow to love and obey him.

But that is not how God designed marriage to be. God doesn't want the man to lord over his wife. The scripture says, "How can two walk together unless they agree?" (Amos 3:3, NIV). The Word also says, "The husband is to love his wife as Christ loved the church and gave himself for it" (Ephesians 5:25, NIV). "And the wife should submit herself unto her own husband as he follows Christ" (Ephesians 5:22, NIV).

Toward the end of October, I had been to the doctor for some female problems and had to have major surgery. The night before I had to go the hospital, Robert and I had another argument. I can't even remember what it was about, but he went to work that evening mad. He got off early the next morning to take me to the hospital, and when we arrived, he just dropped me off at the hospital door. He didn't stay with me because he said he was tired and wanted to get some sleep so he could go to work later that evening.

My mother met me at the hospital. She was there while I had surgery, and she met me in my room after I went through recovery. I was in the hospital for four days, and Robert didn't come to see me until I was about to get out.

He called and said that he was sick. He had a bad infection that made his face swell. He was taking antibiotics, and didn't want to come to the hospital when he looked like a monster. When he came to pick me up, his face was indeed swollen, but I was still hurt that my husband didn't seem to care that I needed and wanted him to show me that I was his priority.

The Journey Down the First Hill

When I came home from the hospital, we picked up speed on our downward journey.

I got home and found that he had been smoking weed a lot more. He was smoking every day and drinking all week long. I was hurt and angry. His lack of support was really starting to affect our relationship. I was beginning to realize that I wasn't his priority and started questioning why he even married me. What about the vow that says, "In sickness and in health"? Well, I was sick and I needed someone to take care of me. I wanted that someone to be my husband. But he didn't seem to be concerned with my health.

We continued to argue about every little thing, like him going out and not spending time with me, the kids (his kids and mine), his not going to church, money, and bills.

I was getting tired of arguing about everything; it was like he turned into a different person. He was short-tempered and angry all the time. He had mood swings and went from one extreme to another. One minute he seemed happy and calm, and then the next minute he was mad and upset because someone called and bothered him about something. He acted like everything bad that was happening was my fault. And he took his anger out on me by yelling and screaming at me.

About two weeks after my surgery, we got into another argument because he had stayed out all night. But this time the argument got really out of control.

Robert had been pretty quiet and withdrawn all week. But at the end of the week, it was another one of those Friday nights.

Robert was getting ready to go out like he did every Friday. He had been drinking, but he was quieter than usual. He wasn't really saying a lot, and I could tell there was something on his mind. I just didn't know what. So I didn't say anything while he was getting ready, and he didn't say anything when he left. I was hurt, angry, and tired of it all. I couldn't understand why I was getting the silent treatment. I was trying to make sense of what was going on. Why was my husband so distant? Is he not interested in me anymore, or was there another woman?

I wanted to leave, but it was my house. I decided I wasn't the one with the problem; I should not be the one to leave.

When Robert went out that night, I didn't chase after him. He just left, and I let him go. My kids were spending the night with my parents, so I was home alone. All night I rehearsed in my head what I was going to say to him when he got home.

Hours went by, and I finally realized he wasn't coming home that night. I didn't get much sleep and kept waking up to see what time it was.

When Robert came in the next morning around 9:00 A.M., I was so mad. I told him we needed to talk. Of course, he didn't want to hear anything I had to say. He started taking off his clothes to get into bed.

I asked him, "What was going on"? He was silent.

I started crying and telling him how much I loved him. and how he was acting like I wasn't even there. He said, "Janice, leave me alone. I don't want to talk about it."

I just couldn't leave it alone. I wanted him to give me answers. He threw the covers off, got out of bed, and started putting his clothes back on. He started cursing at me and saying he was tired of me nagging him all the time. That was his excuse for not coming home. He was leaving.

I was confused. What did he mean? He was tired of my nagging, but we hardly even talked anymore. I was determined we were going to have a discussion. As he got his stuff and headed to the door, I was yelling that I was fed-up and tired of the same old thing week-after-week, and we needed to talk right now. I threatened that if he left, he couldn't come back because I was through with him.

He didn't say a word, but just kept walking toward the door.

I didn't want him to leave, so I followed him down the steps, and I stepped in front of the door to block him from leaving. He got very angry and grabbed me and shoved me into the door. Then he hit me in the head and told me that I could not make him do anything because he was the man. Despite my surgery two weeks prior and my stitches, he picked me up and threw me onto the couch, which was across the room. He said he was tired of my BS, and he left.

I was left dazed and in pain.

My body hurt from the fight and from the stitches. I had a black eye. I knew I needed to call someone, but I didn't want to call my parents or my brother. I didn't want them to see me like this, and I didn't want to get them upset. I finally called a girlfriend, who happened to be a nurse. She came by and made sure that I didn't need medical attention. My face was bruised, and I was an emotional wreck.

I decided I was not going to deal with him hitting me, especially after surgery. His actions did not show sensitivity, consideration, or love.

When he came back that evening, I told him he had to leave, because I was not going to be his punching bag. He did not object or argue. Actually, he only came back to get his clothes. I found out later he had been looking for his own place. Since I was pressing the issue regarding his distance, he felt he could not keep his plan to leave a secret. That is what made him angry.

Once again, I was left to look at what caused another relationship to sour.

The Warnings

Sure, there were warning signs before we got married, but I ignored them. After a few years of dating, although Robert and I weren't living together, he had some of his clothes at my house for the nights or weekends he would stay over. One particular time when I should have paid attention to the warning signs is when we had an argument that turned into a physical fight.

Robert came by one Saturday morning after a night out without me. I told him I could not do this anymore. I was fed up with the Friday nights out and the other women. I wasn't going to keep waiting on the sideline while he had his fun and then decided that it was my turn. So

I started packing his things. He got really mad and flew into a rage. He snatched his clothes out of my hands and pushed me into the bedroom door. He threw me on the bed, while cursing and screaming at me. He was telling me that I had better stop messing (to put it kindly) with him and he was sick of all the BS. He would get his own stuff together when he was ready, and I'd better not touch any of his stuff. He was choking me on the bed while caught up in his rage. It felt like he was "choking me to death." I could not breathe. I was gasping for air and trying to get him off of me. After nearly passing out, he let go of my neck and threw the rest of his clothes into the garbage bag. As he was leaving, I was laying on the bed trying to get some air while he stormed out of the house.

My voice was gone for almost three days. It was Saturday, and I thank God I didn't have any plans while the kids were with my mother. I cried and tried to comprehend what had just happened. I stayed in the house, crawled in the bed, and tried to get myself together. What was I going to tell my mother and children when they came home? My butt was bruised from the doorknob, and I was really sore from being thrown around. No one would see the bruise, so I didn't have to worry about explaining any physical signs of abuse. But what about my voice? I could hardly talk. I decided to just tell people I woke up with a sore throat. It was the truth. When I woke up the next morning, my throat was sore.

A few days later, I found out that when Robert left, he went to his mother's apartment. I tried to call him several times, but he wouldn't talk to me.

Valentine's Day came around soon after that fight, and I decided that I'd go buy him a present. Maybe that would soften him up, and we could work this situation out. I went to the jewelry store, bought him a black onyx ring, and took it over to his mother's house where he was staying. When I first got there, I told him I was sorry for throwing his clothes into a garbage bag. I had done it in anger. I was the one begging him to come back, but he was very cold. He hardly said a word while I was there, but he accepted the ring I had bought. I finally left, feeling hurt and rejected.

Eventually he started calling me. and we got back together. That fight was a major caution sign about what was ahead on this journey we were on together, but I didn't slow down. We got married anyway.

Now, here I was in the same situation again. I thought about why I didn't heed the previous signs—the first physical fight we had with each other, the women, the partying, the drinking, and the staying out all night. Why didn't I stand up and say, "Enough is enough"?

I thought I was in love. The up-and-down roller coaster of emotions went on for five years of dating Robert. I thought the ups and downs were a normal part of relationships. And now. after only four months of marriage, Robert left, and we separated around the first of November.

When Robert left, I cried every day—for seven months. I went to work and church, but all I could think about was that I had failed again. Every day, it felt like I was only going through the motions. I didn't have any energy or life inside of me. In public, I tried to play things off and make everyone think that everything in my life was okay. If someone asked about Robert, I just acted like nothing happened and said that we were just having a hard time. With the exception of my family, I didn't want people to know that we were separated. I felt ashamed and kept trying to make it all make sense in my mind.

All I could really think about was, "Lord, You said You would bless me in my marriage, and I know divorce is not in the will of God." I thought about how I had prayed before I got married. I realized I had prayed to justify what I wanted to do. I tried to make the Word fit, and I kept trying to keep it together on my own.

Although we were separated, Robert called every now and then. I tried to act like I was moving on, but actually it was tearing me up inside. He said he trusted me and knew he could talk to me about anything. It was what I wanted to hear. He was dealing with some personal issues in his family and just needed someone to talk to about it. I listened and was there every time he called. After all, I still loved him. and he was still my husband. I couldn't abandon him when he finally needed me. But at the same time, I had unanswered questions. What about me? What about us? Why do things seem to work out and go smoothly between us when we're not together?

Robert had moved into a townhouse, across from where I lived when I was married to my second husband. We began talking on the phone almost every day. It was like we were starting all over as friends.

On February 14, 1996, Robert called to wish me a Happy Valentine's Day. I jokingly asked if he wanted me to be his valentine. and he said, "Yes." He asked me if I wanted to get together and go out on a date. I did not think about all the warning signs, I was so excited that I agreed. We were still legally married so I thought it was the right thing to do.

The Journey Through the Valley

We went out to a buffet at the casino and spent the evening together talking and laughing. Then we went back to my house and had sex.

A few weeks later I found out I was pregnant. Although I wasn't trying to get pregnant, I wasn't trying not to get pregnant either. This was my husband; I started rationalizing again and thought if we had a child together, things might be different. I love children and wanted to have another child, whether we got back together or not. So when I found out I was pregnant, I called and told him.

He was okay with it at first. He even made it to the first doctor's appointment. However, soon after that he started treating me differently. He stopped calling again and rarely returned my calls. When we did manage to talk, he would say mean things like, I could be in his life, but I could not be his wife. He apologized at later times. and we kept pretending like nothing happened.

But things were not okay at all.

At the end of March, I was at my son's baseball game when I felt something was wrong. I actually felt my baby's life leave my body. I scheduled a sonogram for the next day because I started spotting. I was afraid I was having a miscarriage. On my way to the doctor's office, the

Lord spoke to me and said, "You lost the baby so he could see himself." What did that mean? I did not care about him seeing anything. I was really angry and confused because this was not about him.

I really wanted to have the baby, but God's vision was much greater than mine. When I got to my doctor's appointment, the nurse confirmed the baby's sac collapsed and I miscarried. My emotions were going wild—anger, confusion, more anger and more confusion. I wanted another baby, but the Lord had already decided and actually spoken to me. I did not understand it. I still don't fully understand, but I had to settle it in my heart. Considering that Robert was acting really strangely and becoming distant, it was probably best to not have a child together.

When I got home from the doctor's office, I tried to call and tell him I had lost the baby, but he would not answer the phone. When I finally got in touch with him, he was getting ready for company. I knew that "company" always meant a party or some woman. During our brief conversation over the phone, he told me that he did not love me anymore. Once again he said I could be in his life, but not his wife.

I had heard it before, but with the recent miscarriage of our child, his words ripped my heart into pieces. I was crushed and his nonchalant attitude toward me and what I was going through made me angrier. I just hung up the phone and cried. I paced the floor and yelled out, "How could this man be so insensitive? Doesn't he even care that I just lost his baby?" I felt so helpless and small. I didn't want to talk to him anymore. I had to finally face the fact that the man I loved didn't love me. After hearing him say those words to me again, I finally realized that I was trying to force something that just wasn't going to work.

CHAPTER SIX

OUR JOURNEY ON THE SECOND HILL

April quietly crept in. and I began asking God what I was supposed to do. I told Him I needed to hear from Him because I just couldn't take it anymore. I said, "Lord, I know this is not Your will for me: I know it isn't. So please, show me what to do. I'm tired of trying to make this work on my own. I need Your help and direction. Please speak to my heart so that I'll know what to do."

As I finished praying and crying, I sat quietly on the side of my bed. and the Lord told me, "It is not going to end the way you think." But it didn't make sense. We were already separated. and the only thing I could think of was divorce. I could not imagine any other ending. Nothing else crossed my mind. and I stopped trying to figure it out.

The days were long. and the weeks seemed to creep by. I was praying and seeking God for an answer, every day. On June 9, 1996, I was praying, crying, and laying my heart out before God and pleading, "Lord, I need to hear from You." While I was praying, the Lord told me to go back to the scripture I was given in the beginning—I Corinthians 7:10-16. He told me to read the whole thing. All I had been doing was holding onto part of the promise, because all I wanted to hear was that Robert was going to become a Christian since I was one. That was the justification I needed to marry someone who didn't believe in Christ the way I did. So, I went back and read it all. I took my time reading the scripture I was so familiar with because, obviously, I had missed something. I read each word out loud, and as I was reading, peace came over me, and the words began to jump off the page.

The first part tells how the unbelieving husband is sanctified by the wife, but verse 15 states:

> *"...but if the unbelieving depart, let him depart. A brother or sister is not under bondage in such cases: but God hath called us to peace."*

At that point, it was as if a load or a weight was being lifted off of me. I accepted that Robert didn't have a relationship with God and with the statement he made, over and over again, about me not being his wife, our marriage was not bound spiritually (or in the sight of God). Although we had made a covenant vow to each other when we got married, the bond and the covenant we made were broken because of Robert's behavior. It was just a matter of legally going through the process of getting a divorce.

I felt at peace that Monday in June. My prayer time was strengthening me and helping me get a handle on life. My attention was not directed at what was going wrong, but on how God was helping me to become confident in knowing who I was. I was God's child.

Pulling the Brake

After I had finished praying, the phone rang. I looked at the caller ID and was surprised to see Robert's number. I couldn't imagine what he wanted. He had been ignoring me and hadn't returned my phone calls. Did he want to rub the hurt in my face some more?

I answered the phone. He asked how I was doing. I told him I had been doing a lot of praying and thinking about our situation. He was quiet. I told him, "As soon as I get some money, I am going to file for divorce since you don't want to be married anymore." He didn't have much to say except, "If that's what you want to do, that's fine with me."

At first, I was a little confused. He was acting like this was all my idea and something I wanted. But I just said, "Okay. Well, I'll let you know when I get the money to file for the divorce. I'll talk to you later." I hung up the phone and began to pray even more. I needed to know how I was going to pay for this. I asked God to show me what to do and to tell me how this was going to turn out.

That Wednesday, Robert called and said he had gotten an attorney, filed a petition for divorce, and paid for it. He said he only called to tell me that he needed me to sign the divorce papers so he could take them back to his attorney. When I hung up the phone, I thought to myself, "Wow, look at God. He works fast." I walked through my house rejoicing and thanking God for this miracle. I knelt down in the middle of the floor to pray. and the Lord told me again, "It's not going to end the way you think." But I thought everything was okay. Robert did not seem angry. and in about thirty days we would finally be divorced.

Then I started noticing things.

The Journey into Strange Behaviors

One night I was sitting outside with a guy I knew when I noticed Robert slowly drive by my house. I wondered what he was doing driving by my house, so I waved at him to stop. But he just kept going. Later, he called and made some startling accusations, "Is that the N_____ you're sleeping with?" I told him the man he saw was just a friend. I made a point to tell him, "If I was trying to hide something, don't you think I would be a little more discreet than sitting on the front porch?" He said, "Don't get smart!" He hung up.

As days passed, I went through my normal routine of going to work, church, and back home. On several different occasions, whenever I was leaving the house or sometimes coming home, I saw Robert riding by my house in different cars. He never stopped. though. He would just drive slowly by the house and stare at me while I was in the car either pulling in or out of my driveway. In my mind I questioned, why is he just riding by my house? Was he stalking me? Was he trying to see who was coming in and out of the house? I started to pray even more because I was getting scared of Robert. I didn't understand why he was watching me. But God continued to show me how He loved me and was protecting me.

One day the alarm sensors went out at my house. I called the alarm company to come out and service the system. The technician said I should change the security code since I had used the same code for four years. He asked, "While I am here, do you want me to change it?" Without thinking anything of it I said, "Well, okay, sure."

A week later on June 28, my husband tried to break into my house.

That morning my mom picked my daughter up for summer school as usual. As she was driving away from the house, she saw Robert driving toward the house. She called me at work because it seemed odd. While I was talking to my mother, I got a call from the alarm company telling me my alarm was going off. I immediately left work and headed home while my mom dropped my daughter off at school and went back to the house to sit outside until I got there. Apparently the alarm scared Robert. He wasn't there when my mom got there.

Robert called me later that morning to question me about changing the alarm code. He said I was trying to play him and make him look like a fool. I asked what he was looking for at my house. Stuttering, he said he was looking for … he was looking for some car parts he left. I think he was looking to see if there was any evidence of a man. He was not at all happy that I changed the alarm code. He thought I changed the code because I was afraid of him.

Even though it wasn't my fear that caused me to change the code, I was afraid of him. His behavior changed again. Instead of never calling me, he began calling regularly. But, now he was making threats.

He called and stayed silent, which was quite disturbing. Or he would say things like, "You better watch yourself," and "Who do you think you are?" Then he would just hang up. He called a couple of times in the middle of the night and told me, "I could do things to hurt you. and no one would ever know." I was moving from just plain scared to terrified, but I didn't want to tell anyone. I didn't want to think, "This guy is crazy, and he might really hurt me." I dismissed the threats and decided he must be smoking and drinking more than usual. I thought, "He's the one that wants out of this marriage. He's told me repeatedly that I can't be his wife anymore. He is just drunk and doesn't really mean it. Why would someone I love want to hurt me?"

The calls continued. and he even started calling me at my job with threatening messages. I had to get my supervisor involved. He was calling so much it was a distraction. and I wasn't getting much work done. Things did not get better. They got much worse. I had to keep my mind on what I heard in my prayer time. Once again God told me, "It will not end the way you think."

"I never dreamed that ..."

CHAPTER SEVEN

THE JOURNEY NIGHTMARE

Robert, the man I vowed to cherish and love forever…"'til death do us part," tested every part of our wedding vows. Little did I know, my life was about to change forever.

Round One: The Assault

It was Monday evening, July 1, 1996, when Robert called and said, "I have the divorce papers, and I want you to sign them. So, can you come by?" My mind quickly thought about all the threatening phone calls and how he drove by my house as though he was stalking me. I said to myself, "I am not going over there tonight." He tried to get me to come by that evening, but I just didn't think it was a good idea. I told him it was too late and that I would stop by his place in the morning since I passed his complex on my way to work. He finally agreed to that plan. I asked him if he would bring the papers out to the car when I got there. He said, "Yeah, okay," and hung up the phone.

The next morning I called Robert to let him know that I was on my way to his house. I pulled up in front of his complex and honked the horn, but he did not come out. I started to get nervous, but I ignored the feeling and went up to his door. I was nervous because before I left home, the Holy Ghost told me to call my mom to tell her what I was doing. But I didn't call.

The kids had stayed with my mother. It was early, and I didn't want to worry her with the knowledge that Robert had been threatening me and asked for a divorce. I just wasn't ready to answer a lot of questions. Besides, I never thought I would have any problems.

Ignoring my fear, I went to the door, rang the doorbell, and went inside when he answered. I was nervous and frustrated because Robert told me on the phone that he'd bring the papers out to me. As I stood in the doorway, he told me to wait a minute while he went to get the papers. He went into the kitchen, but came back into the front room empty handed. He said they must be upstairs, and motioned for me just to wait while he went upstairs. He appeared to be looking for the papers, but as I stood in the doorway waiting, I got the feeling that he was stalling. He was upstairs for about five minutes before he came back down the steps. When he reached the bottom of the stairs, I noticed that he didn't have anything in his hands.

Suddenly he slapped me, and I fell across the couch. When I got up, I realized my lip was deeply cut and bruised. Then, he started choking and cursing at me. He said, "You can't leave me because I'm the man in charge." He kept choking and slapping me.

He reached under the pillow on the couch, pulled out a handgun, and put it up to my head.

"I am going to kill you," he yelled.

I was in shock and tremendous pain. I just knew I was going to die.

As I sat there in shock and disbelief, I heard the Holy Ghost say, "*It is not your time*."

I began thinking—if it is not my time, what is going to happen here?

As I sat crying on the couch, holding my face, Robert was pacing screaming, cursing, and waving the gun in the air. Occasionally, he stopped, pointed the gun right at me, and yelled, "You think you're calling the shots? You're not. Look at what you've done! You can't just decide you're going to leave me. Tell me who's calling the shots?"

I was so scared; I just sat there and watched every move he made while hoping he wasn't going to shoot the gun.

As he continued in his rage, he walked over to the front closet and pulled out a shotgun. He opened the barrel and loaded it with five shells. He put it to my chest and said sarcastically, "Oh, you are so holy. A Christian woman—are you ready to meet your maker? You believe in God so much. So are you ready to go to heaven? Call on God, now."

I thought, "Okay, Lord, You said it is not my time. So now what?"

I braced myself, trying to imagine what it would feel like to get shot and have an awfully big hole in my chest. I believed and knew I was not going to die, but I thought I would be paralyzed for the rest of my life.

Robert was hollering and asking me questions like, "Don't you love me?" and "Why are you trying to hurt me like all the other women that I've been in love with?" He kept talking about how much he loved me. Then I started to get angry, thinking, "What am I supposed to say here? How do I respond to that?" He had the handgun at my head, and the shotgun at my chest. Finally, I told him I could not say anything with him yelling about killing me and with him pointing the guns at me.

After what seemed like hours of Robert pacing back and forth, yelling, and cursing at me, he began to calm down. Robert put the guns down and strangely enough, he started crying. He cried while softly saying how much he loved me. I whispered, "This is not love."

I sat on the couch, watching this man unravel emotionally. He said, "Where's your wedding ring"? As I held out my hand to show him, he told me to take it off and give it to him. He said, "You've broken your vows to me, so don't think that you're going to keep this ring."

As I took the ring off my finger, he yelled, "Put it back on." So I put the ring back on.

Then he said, "You're like all the rest of the women because you thought you could use me. I thought you were different."

Then he made me take the ring off. But again, no sooner had I taken it off, he yelled, "Put it back on!"

I was confused because I had never seen Robert like this. Where was all this craziness coming from?

I asked God, "How am I getting out of this?"

Suddenly, he calmed down completely. He took me upstairs and told me to undress. My heart was beating so fast not knowing what he was going to do. He told me to lie down on the bed. He unbuckled his pants and pulled them down. He climbed on top of me. He started raping me.

I just cried.

He asked, "What are you crying for? I am your husband. This is what we are supposed to do."

All I could say was, "This is not love. This is not how you treat someone you love."

He lifted my legs and whispered in my ear to move my body. Tears rolled down my face, and I did what he said. I closed my eyes and just kept thinking, "Just do what he says and maybe he'll let me go."

He asked me over and over if I missed him. He asked me, "Doesn't this feel good?"

I could hardly speak, but managed to say, "This isn't love."

He finally got up and told me to get dressed. I got up slowly and put my underwear on. Every part of my body was shaking as I sat on the side of the bed sobbing.

It was about 8:30 in the morning. I had been there almost three hours.

Suddenly, I thought about my mom. I told him, "My mom calls me every morning at work. She's probably worried since she hasn't heard from me. My boss is probably wondering if something is wrong too because I did not call in." I begged, "Please let me go. I will not tell anybody, if you just let me go. I'm going to work, and no one will have to know about this."

Robert said, "Go wash up, put your clothes on, and go downstairs. You know, I don't know why I'm letting you go. Are you sure you are not going to tell anyone?"

I assured him, "No, I am not going to say a word."

He repeated, "I don't know why I am doing this, but I am going to let you go if you go straight to work."

After nearly three hours of horror, Robert opened the door, and I walked out of his apartment. I walked quickly to my car, praying he wouldn't change his mind and make me go back inside. I didn't even turn around to see if he was watching me. I just got into my car and slowly pulled off. I was trying to stay calm, so he would not think I was panicking. I didn't know if he was going to follow me, so I went straight to work. I had a badly bruised lip, a black eye, and bruises on my neck.

Round Two: The Official Complaint

Once I got to work, I just broke down crying and called my girlfriend, Saundra, over to my desk. She looked at my face and quickly took me into an empty office. I told her what happened, and she told me she was going to call my twin brother, John. I gave Saundra John's number. She called him and said I was hurt pretty badly by Robert and that he needed to come down to the office to get me.

While we waited for John to arrive, the HR Director came in and suggested that I go to a shelter for battered women. She asked for my permission to call a shelter so I could at least get some help and information about domestic violence. I told her I would take the information, and while she went to her office to get the telephone number to the shelter, my supervisor came in to see if I was okay. I was so ashamed to involve so many people in my situation. I was embarrassed that people on my job now knew what I was going through.

As I waited in the office for my brother, I thought about Daimon, who was sixteen, and Taukia, who was eleven. I decided I did not want to leave my house, uproot my children, or go to a strange, unfamiliar place at such an emotional time. My children were already at my mother's house, so they could stay there safely while I dealt with everything.

I talked to a counselor at Rose Brooks Domestic Violence Center in Kansas City, MO. She tried to persuade me to come to the shelter, but I refused. She explained to me the cycle of abuse: how it all starts out as verbal or emotional torment, and how so many women don't pay attention to the warning signs of an abuser. She urged me to go and file charges against him, get an Order of Protection, and not to deal with the situation alone. She said, "That is what an abuser wants—for the person who is being abused to be silent. Usually the perpetrator will come back and try to hurt you again. If they do it once, they will do it again." She warned me, I was not safe by myself. I should move to a safer place until I went to court or had him arrested."

After the conversation with the counselor, I called one of my girlfriends who lived alone and asked if I could stay with her for awhile. That was my first step in ending the cycle of violence.

When my brother John arrived at my office, he looked at me and asked what happened. He saw the bruises and my busted lip. He didn't say a lot, but I knew he was upset. I got my things together, and he took me to the courthouse to file for an "Order of Protection" against Robert.

As I walked into the courthouse, I was nervous and embarrassed. I was hoping that I didn't run into anyone I knew. I didn't want them to see my face all bruised up. But ironically, as we got off the elevator and walked into the "Domestic Violence" complaint office area, Robert's sister was working at the office next door. She happened to be sitting at the front desk talking with her mother. As I walked into the area, Robert's mother turned, looked at me, and said out loud, "Oh my God, I can't have another son go to jail." She never asked me what happened or was I okay—nothing.

I was shocked by his mother's comment, and I couldn't say a word. I couldn't believe all she thought about was her son going to jail.

John told me he would be in the waiting area while I went in to file the paperwork. So, in hurt and disbelief, I walked into the office to file an "official" complaint. I say "official" because when Robert tried to break into my house on June 28, I went to the courthouse to file a complaint, but the person on duty told me, "Because there was no physical evidence, it would probably not get approved, since it's his word against yours." Back then I said, "Oh, I have to either get killed or badly hurt to prove to you all that somebody is after me or wanting to hurt me." The clerk said, "I am sorry. I am just letting you know you can file it, but it probably will not get approved. It is your word against his."

As I walked into the office on Tuesday July 2, the lady who helped me the previous Friday was sitting at the desk. I walked up to her and said, "Here is your proof."

She looked at me and seemed to be a little startled, but then seemed to recognize me from Friday. She pulled out the form I started on Friday. I was surprised she still had it right on her desk. I think she felt sorry for me because she wouldn't look at me.

She took me into a small room and told me to have a seat. She asked me to finish filing the complaint and write out the details of what happened. She took a few pictures of my face and neck, and then placed them in the file. We went back to her desk, and she told me the court date was set for July 11, 1996. Without any emotion she explained what happened next in the process. Robert would know I broke my promise to stay silent when served with papers to appear in court.

On the way home from the courthouse, I asked John if he would take me out to stay with my friend Yevonne. I told him the Rose Brook counselor suggested I go somewhere more safe, somewhere Robert couldn't find me. The counselor told me, "Once abusers are served with legal papers, they usually get angry at the victim. It would be best if you weren't alone." John took me to my house to get some clothes. I called my mother and asked if the kids could stay with her for a few weeks or at least until I went to court. My mother and brother agreed it was a good idea. I packed the kids some clothes for John to take back with him after he dropped me off.

When I got to Vonnie's house, I called the kids and talked to them. I explained the need for them to stay with Grandma for a few weeks. I didn't go into a lot of detail because I didn't want them to worry or become afraid. They didn't ask any questions. It was summertime, and they enjoyed being at Grandma's house.

I got settled in at Vonnie's. I was so tired, I went straight to bed.

As I lay there, I began to cry and think about everything that was happening. It was so overwhelming and hurtful. I thought to myself, "I shouldn't be in a situation like this! What's wrong with me?" I tried to close my eyes, but I just kept seeing this vision of Robert and then I would hear, "It's not going to end the way you think." I couldn't seem to get those words out of my head. I knew I had to do something.

I didn't know what to do, but I knew that I had to get a plan together. I thought, "I've got to protect myself and my children." It was a scary time because I didn't know what was going to happen from day to day. I went to work, to my mother's house, and then to Vonnie's house. A few times I went by my house to make sure no one had broken in and that everything was still in order.

Even though I was trying to be as careful as I could, there were times I saw Robert riding around my mom's or my house. He was still stalking me. I didn't know what to do because he didn't stop or say anything to me; he just stared at me as he drove by. I became very cautious about being outside because I lived in fear.

Round Three: The Judgment

Finally, the day came for me to go to court. My father and brother took me so I wouldn't have to go alone. My mother stayed home because she didn't want to hear all the details. She also had to take Taukia to summer school and Daimon to work.

We got to the courthouse early and sat toward the back. My father and brother sat on both sides of me. This was the first time I'd ever been in court for domestic violence. I was surprised there were so many people present, dealing with the same thing. I didn't realize this was happening to so many women.

Robert came in with his sister and brother-in-law and sat on the opposite side of the courtroom. Fear gripped me when he walked in, making me nervous. I tried not to pay him any attention, so I just kept looking forward. The time seemed to drag on, and the judge was calling everyone else before she finally called our names to hear our case.

When we stood up before the judge, Robert tried to turn everything around and said I was chasing him. He told the judge a bunch of lies about me harassing him, calling him all the time, and riding by his house. While he was telling the judge his side of the story, he handed her papers showing her that he had filed the divorce papers. I thought to myself, "Are these the same papers he did not have the morning I went to his house?" I realized the papers had just been a ploy to get me over to his house, because he told the judge he picked the papers up from his attorney and signed them before he came to court that morning.

He kept repeating to the judge, "See, I have already filed for divorce. I do not want her." The judge looked the papers over and flipped through the court file and saw the pictures then she asked me what happened and why was I there.

I told her about his breaking into my house; calling my job with threats; and how he called me and said he wanted me to come by to sign the divorce papers. But when I got there, he couldn't seem to find them. He hit me and pulled the guns out; he threatened to kill me. I told her he took me upstairs in his apartment and raped me. I told her I begged him to let me go and after about three hours, he did. She sat there a few minutes, while Robert kept interrupting and yelling that I was lying. She finally asked Robert, "Well, if she is lying, you will not have a problem staying away from her then, will you?" He said, "Nah, nah. I do not want to be bothered with her, and I want you to keep her away from me." The judge said she had heard enough. She granted the protection order.

As we left the courtroom, Robert told me that I had better not come near him. My brother told me just to keep walking and not to respond. As we were standing and waiting for the elevator, Robert made a smart remark to John and told him he better watch his back. John said, "Man I'm not scared of you. Say whatever you want, but you won't be bothering my sister any more. We all know what's going on, and it ain't a secret anymore." I was really scared, because now Robert was threatening my brother, too! And John doesn't back down. I didn't want anything like a fight to break out right there in the courthouse. The elevator came, Robert got on, and we waited for the next one.

John drove me back to Vonnie's house, and I stayed with her a few more days. But I didn't like living in fear. I decided I was going to move back into my house. I thought, "I am not going to let this man run me out of my house."

I moved back home while the kids stayed with my family. I did not want to endanger them by bringing them home. I figured I'd let things cool down, and hopefully Robert would leave me alone.

Round Four: The Hostage Situation

The first few days back home were pretty quiet. I went to work, went to see the kids, and then went back home.

On Thursday, July 18, I went by my mother's house to pick up Daimon to take him to work at the grocery store. My mother and Taukia rode along, and we stopped off to get some ice cream before returning to my mother's house. Taukia wanted to stay with me until it was time to go back and get Daimon from work. So, after I dropped Mom off at her house, Taukia and I went home. I wanted to spend some time with her, and I had to get some more clothes for them to take back over to my mother's house.

After we had been home for a while, my mother called and said she was missing some important papers. She thought she had left them in my car and was sending John over to check. Meanwhile, a couple of Daimon's friends came by to see him. I told them Daimon was at work, but while they were there, I went out to see if my mom's papers were in the car. I thought it was safe to be outside while the boys were there.

I stood in the driveway with my back to the street and looked around in the car. I found the papers in the trunk. How they got there is still a mystery to me. As I got the papers out of the trunk, I was chatting with the boys sitting on the front steps. While we were talking, one of the boys turned and said, "Hey, what's up?" I thought, "Why is he asking 'what's up' in the middle of the conversation?" But then I realized he was talking to someone behind me. I turned around and froze as Robert walked up into my driveway with a gun in his hand.

We all froze when Robert raised the gun and threatened to shoot. He told the boys to leave and they immediately got up and headed toward their car. I cried out, "Please, don't leave! If you do, he is going to kill me." The boys were scared because Robert waved the gun around and threatened to shoot them, too, so they jumped into the car and left. As they backed out of the driveway, I began to cry and pray that they would go somewhere to call the police.

As the boys drove away, Robert grabbed my arm and pulled me toward the front door. I screamed, "Help! Somebody call the police. Call the police!" I tried to get someone's attention, anyone's attention! My house was on the corner in a very quiet neighborhood. Everyone in the subdivision kept to themselves, but we looked out for each other. Although I lived on a main street, usually people passing by my house were those who lived in the subdivision. There wasn't a lot of traffic in or out. I thought and prayed someone would pass by in a car, hear me, or see us struggling and would stop to help me. But, no one drove up or down the street. Once again, I just knew I was getting ready to die.

Robert yelled and waved the gun at me. He wanted me to go inside the house, but I didn't want to go inside. My daughter, Taukia, was in the house. She was only eleven-years-old, and I hadn't really prepared her for something like this.

Robert fired a gunshot into the air. I saw Taukia looking out her bedroom window as Robert grabbed me again and tried to force me to go into the house. I only hoped Taukia would think to call 911. I struggled with him and fell to the ground. He hit me in the head with the butt of the gun. I heard a "crack," and blood went everywhere. The force from the hit caused all three layers of skin to break and busted my head open. Blood shot out of my head like a faucet had been turned on. I was, literally, covered from head to toe. I was dazed as he grabbed me by my hair and dragged me into the house.

As I looked up at Robert, I couldn't believe my eyes. I actually saw a demon as I looked at him. Robert's head was swollen; his eyes were protruding; and he had these knots on his face. He wasn't himself, nor did he look like himself. He was full of rage and had this blank look in his eyes. I started praying, "Lord, two weeks ago You said it was not my time. Is it my time, now?" The Lord said, "Just be still."

As I lay on the floor crying, Taukia stood at the top of the stairs and saw me covered in blood. She became hysterical and started crying and screaming, "Don't kill my mother." She must have thought Robert had shot me because I was covered with blood. I pleaded with Robert, "Let Taukia go. You don't want her to remember you like this. You know she thinks of you as her father. Don't let her have these memories of you. Please let her go."

Between my pleading and Taukia's crying, Robert finally opened the front door and told her to go outside. She was still crying and screaming for me, but I tried to assure her that I would be okay and she should get out of the house. She finally walked outside, and Robert closed the door behind her. I could only pray that she would go to the neighbor's house across the street and tell them what was going on, but I had no way of knowing what she would do, or whether I would see her again.

In the meantime, I didn't know that Daimon's friends had rushed to his job at the grocery store and told him what was happening. Daimon called the police.

I could hear Taukia standing outside the door crying, and then, suddenly, the police knocked on the door and announced their presence.

The officer yelled, "We need to talk to the owner of the house. We received a call that someone needs our assistance." Robert wouldn't open the door, and the officer tried to get him to come out of the house. Instead, Robert was getting agitated, and he fired the gun at the door a couple of times. The police called an "Operation 100"—hostage situation.

They roped off the house and blocked off the streets. No one could come near the house or drive onto the block, and nobody in the surrounding houses could leave. The police did not know what Robert was going to do.

I sat on the floor wondering if the bullets Robert shot through the door hit anyone like my daughter or the police officer. For awhile, there was only silence. I put my head in my hands and began to cry.

Robert took me up to my bedroom and pushed me down. He said, "Sit down while I think." As I sat on the side of the bed, blood was still running down my face, and I was in a lot of pain.

Robert was so irrational. One minute he was angry, yelling and screaming at me that I had caused all this mess. Then the next minute he acted as though he was sorry he hurt me. He tried to clean me up, and he tried to dress my wound. I had blood all over my face and clothes. It seemed as though the bleeding wouldn't stop. He took me to the bathroom, handed me a towel, and told me to wash up as he went down to the kitchen to get some ice for my head. I felt so dirty.

As I looked in the mirror I thought to myself, "How could this happen to me—the nice girl raised in the Methodist Church who went to Catholic school all her life? All kinds of thoughts and pictures went through my mind. As I washed my face and arms, I thought to myself, "How did I get here? Does my family know what's going on? Will I get out of this alive? I'm only 34-years-old. I have two children to finish raising. They already don't have their fathers in their lives, so they can't lose me, too. What would they do? How would they feel?" Tears ran down my face as I continued to think to myself, "Boy, I have made so many mistakes, and my children are the ones that are suffering the consequences." I had been so selfish for putting my desire for a man over my children's safety and well-being. I realized all the relationships I'd been in weren't healthy for my children or me. But I had wanted my dream more than I wanted to face reality. I did whatever I thought was best to make my dream a reality. I had not considered the cost! What was wrong with me? Where did I go wrong? What made me make the same mistakes over and over again? Was it too late to change my thinking and what I wanted? Was it too late for me? Was this the end?"

Robert came back upstairs with a bag of ice and watched as I tried to clean myself up. He saw me crying and said, "Stop crying so your head will stop bleeding!"

I got as much blood off my body and clothes as I could, then Robert took me back into the bedroom. My head was hurting, and I sat quietly on the side of the bed.

Then the phone rang. Robert answered it and started talking to one of his sisters. I didn't know what they were saying, but I heard Robert say, "She's all right." They talked a few minutes more, and then he hung up the phone. Different members of his family started calling on the telephone, which made me wonder if they knew what he was doing. My mom called because by the time John got close to the house to look for the papers he was stopped by the police and all the yellow crime scene tape. The phone kept ringing with different people calling to talk to Robert and make sure I was okay. His family talked to him, then talked to me to ask if I was okay. I thought it was strange that Robert let me talk to everyone who called, but I was very careful about what I said to them, and how I responded to their questions.

Because of the head trauma, I felt like I was going to pass out. Robert walked me so that I stayed awake. He put ice on my wound to stop the bleeding and swelling. But at the same time, I could tell that he was getting really nervous. He decided we needed to get out of the house and go somewhere no one could find us. Somewhere he could think and finish what he came there to do. But when he opened the door, the police put the spotlight on us. He grabbed me and put me in front of him, as a human shield. He realized they had the place surrounded. He quickly closed the door.

We heard the S.W.A.T. team on the roof and in the yard. We saw the infrared beams shining through the windows. He was trying to find a safe place in the house away from the police. Robert was getting more and more nervous. He said he had to think. I guess, he originally thought he had it all planned out. It was going to be quick. Nobody would know until it was too late. But it didn't play out the way he had planned. He was feeling trapped and like he had no way out. He had no new plan for this situation. What had he done?

Robert's behavior became more and more erratic. One minute he was calm and seemingly rational, the next he was angry, even volatile, toward me.

He thought the basement was the safest spot from the police, so he took me downstairs. While we were in the basement, he took advantage of me sexually. I was confused and didn't understand how someone could have or would want to have sex at a time like this. It was so degrading, and I felt so disgusted because I was on my monthly cycle. Robert didn't get satisfied so he told me to get on my knees and made me perform oral sex. I gagged repeatedly, almost throwing up. As he stood over me, he kept asking, "What's wrong?" All I could say was how disgusting it all was. I asked, "How could you make me do this?" He said, "Well, we are still husband and wife." I began to cry and told him, "If you love me, you wouldn't be doing this to me. This is not the way you treat someone you say you love." He pushed me back and pulled up his pants.

We only stayed in the basement for a short period of time because we could hear the police outside in the yard. We moved from the family room, on the lower level of the house, up to the stairway leading to the bedrooms. I guess Robert thought the police could not just shoot into the house and kill him with multiple walls on each side.

The phone had not rung for awhile, but suddenly, as we sat on the stairs, it rang again. This time it was a police negotiator.

I couldn't hear what the negotiator was saying, but I assumed he was trying to talk Robert out of the house and convince him to let me go and surrender. I kept hearing Robert say things like, "You need to back off and let us get in the car and leave," and "She's okay, she's sitting right here." I guess they weren't telling Robert what he wanted to hear, so he got mad and hung up.

After a few minutes of silence, the phone rang again. This time the negotiator must have promised Robert something if he could talk to me. Robert handed me the phone and said, "Tell them you're okay." The officer said, "Just listen while I ask you a few questions and respond with "Yes" or "No." Interrupt me if Robert starts moving around, and I'll ask me another question so we can try to assess the situation in there."

The officer asked, "Are you hurt?"

I replied, "Yes."

Then he asked, "Are you in one of the bedrooms?

And I replied, "No."

"Are you in the basement?"

"No."

"Where are you hurt?"

"My head."

"Are you bleeding right now?"

"No."

He asked, "Are you and Robert sitting on the stairs?"

I said, "Yes."

"Are you on the stairs going up?"

"Yes."

Robert grabbed the phone and said, "That's enough." Robert asked the negotiator if he was satisfied. Then Robert said the next time he called back he'd better be telling him that they are letting us leave. Robert hung up the phone.

The time seemed to drag on so slow. All I could think to do was to pray quietly.

Because God told me a few weeks ago, "It wasn't my time," I believed I wasn't going to die. This comfort gave me courage.

I started to get bold and a little impatient. I worked up enough guts and asked, "Can we go?" while I looked at my watch.

"Girl," he said, "You are crazy. Don't you see what is happening? Neither one of us is leaving this house."

I said, "All they want to know is that I am alright. They know I am bleeding. They just want us to come out. Neither one of us has to die."

He told me to shut up. He was agitated because the negotiator kept calling. It is stressful to ignore a ringing phone.

After a few hours, I asked if he was really going to kill me.

He said, "If I have to. Neither one of us is leaving this house alive."

So, while we were still on the steps, I asked Robert if I could pray. I said, "If you are going to shoot me, let me pray."

As I turned to kneel, he added, "Well, say a prayer for me."

"Okay," I sighed.

I prayed to myself, "Lord, I'm sorry for all that I've done; for being disobedient and for going against Your Word. You told me that it's not my time, and I don't know how I'm going to get out of this, but You do. Please forgive Robert and have mercy on him." I had peace within myself that I can't explain. I just knew inside that I was going to live to see another day.

After what seemed to be hours, we were startled to hear a key unlocking the front door. I sat with my eyes wide open. Robert was on the phone with the negotiator, with the gun still in his hand. He got real nervous and jumpy.

He told the negotiator, with his voice rising, "If you do not call them off, I am going to kill her. I AM GOING TO KILL HER!" The door was now unlocked, and the doorknob turned.

As the door opened, Robert dropped the phone and put his left hand down toward my head, I guess to feel where I was. He pointed the gun at me, and I braced myself.

As he stood up, instead of shooting me, he pointed the gun at the door and fired. Two police officers busted in and stood right in front of us. They told him to put down the gun.

Robert fired another shot.

The police started shooting.

The end happened so fast.

I was still sitting at the bottom of the stairs—shocked. As I sat there staring at the two officers in front of me, I heard the Spirit inside of me say, "Move out of the way, fool. You are in the line of fire." Bullets flew over my head. I rolled over to the side, and one of the officers dove and fell over me.

After the shooting stopped, the officer helped me up and led me outside. I looked around as the officer took me to the ambulance, but things just didn't seem real. Officers were coming from different directions toward the house with more guns. The paramedics helped me up into the ambulance and bandaged my head to stop the bleeding. I looked around to see if they were going to bring Robert out behind me.

They didn't bring my husband out.

CHAPTER EIGHT

THE AFTERMATH

I couldn't see or hear anything. I wanted to know what was happening inside the house. I asked the paramedic, "Is he dead?" For a long time neither of the paramedics said anything. After asking over and over, one of the paramedics nodded yes.

Every part of me went numb, and everything around me seemed so distant. The noises around me stopped. Everyone and everything moved in slow motion. Then I closed my eyes and remembered—the vision.

It seemed so long ago, but the vision I had when I stayed at my girlfriend's house had now come to pass.

I remembered lying in her bed and I saw Robert's body jerking as though he was being shot. He was in a white T-shirt, blue jeans, and tennis shoes. I told the Lord then, I did not want anyone to die.

The Lord said, "It is going to be his choice. You can either get in the way and get hurt or stay out of the way."

I just threw my hands up and said, "I surrender, Lord, to Your will."

It was not God's will for Robert to die. Not under these circumstances or in this way. I can image the sadness the Lord felt knowing that Robert chose death over life. He didn't give his life to Christ. It happened just as God said it would; it was Robert's choice.

He shot at the police first, knowing they are trained to come in and kill. He could have surrendered, allowing both of us to live.

It was amazing how God revealed the future through that vision.

The day Robert died, jerking at the top of the steps, he had on the same clothes I saw in that vision.

It was finally over. Surely, it did not end the way I thought it would.

It was well after midnight when I was taken to the hospital where they stitched up my head. Because I was sedated, I don't remember a lot about the ride to the hospital or being at the hospital, except that the police came and took pictures of me and my clothes. I do remember my son and his friends in the emergency room. My son leaned over and kissed me and held my hand as the nurses and doctors came in and out of the room. Robert's oldest son, Robert (or Monte' as we called him), was one of Daimon's best friends. And Monte's mother, Kathy, and I had also become good friends, so it was not surprising to see her walk into the emergency room. Kathy and her cousin came to see about me, and she seemed relieved to know that I was still alive. Her coming to see about me and genuinely caring really meant a lot to me. Her son had just lost his father, and here she was checking on the person who others would blame for his death.

Later the police took me to the police station to get my statement. My mom, daughter, and son were there, too. The officers told me my daughter was a big help to them because she had given them a layout of the house. She told them where each room was and explained where things were in case they had to go inside. It was a heart-wrenching experience for my children and me. We were devastated and drained.

When we finally got home late Friday morning, I needed closure. I wanted to go to my house and see what happened. My mother didn't want me to go to my house because she was afraid that it was too soon for me to have to deal with what I would see when I got there. She refused to take me, so I went to sleep for a while.

Later on Friday evening, I asked my father if he would take me to my house, and he did.

When we arrived, the house was wide open. Since the police busted in and Robert shot at the door, the police took the door off the hinges to be processed as evidence.

When I went in, I saw the pool of blood where Robert's body fell. There were about twenty chalk marks around the bullet holes in my room, my daughter's room, the hallway, and on the carpet.

Standing there motionless, I realized I would never forget what I went through in the name of "love."

So many emotions were going through my mind, I cannot begin to explain or sort them all out. It is something I never wanted to experience, and something I wish I could prevent from happening to anyone else.

What woman thinks on the day that she utters those vows and dreams it will be so glorious that it could end in such tragedy? But it didn't end there.

"I never could have dreamed this…"

PART TWO

APPLICATIONS FROM THE AUTHOR

Addressing Relationship Regret

If I would have known before I said, "I do," what I learned in the process or after, would my answer be different? I don't know. I think I would have been more cautious—taken more time for me instead of him. Or would I?

Some experiences get us to the point God wants us to be. No, I did not want anyone to die, but that experience changed how I thought about myself, how I viewed men, and how I approached relationships.

I will never say what I will not do. But I am daily praying I stay so close to God that I will never endure another relationship like that one or involve myself with a man who is not seeking God first for himself and then for his wife.

Wisdom for Commitment

Just because a person goes to church doesn't mean they have an intimate relationship with God, the One who created us and loves us unconditionally. As we study and learn from the Word of God, we should remember, all men in church are not seeking the face of God. And all women at the altar are not necessarily praying, but they may be preying.

We have to be honest with ourselves and responsible for our actions and the choices we make. We must realize that our choices always effect someone other than just ourselves. Past experience with things or people is the best teacher on how to handle our future relationships because they show us where we could have done things different or better. They also help us to realize who we are and what our strengths and weaknesses are. From those, we learn balance, and that's how we grow.

We have to learn to love ourselves first and listen to wise counsel. Growing up, we think we have it all figured out, and that our parents or other people who may have gone through a similar situation, just don't understand. But we couldn't be more wrong in our thinking. I once heard that the word "History" really means "His Story." When we have examples from people's lives and from the Holy Bible to give us a roadmap, why do we think that it will be different when it comes to us? The scripture says in Ecclesiastes 1:9 (NIV), "What has been will be again, what has been done will be done again; there is nothing new under the sun." The faces are different, and the names may change, but I guarantee that someone has gone through what you're dealing with right now.

We can't rush God's will. Instead, we should seek His perfect will, not His permissive or acceptable will, because those are available, too. When we truly want something, whether it's good or bad, we often make up our mind and start finding ways to get it. In reality, the first thing we should do is ask God what His will is concerning our desire or request. Then WAIT for His answer. That's where the problem usually comes in. Although we ask God to give us the answer to something particular, we usually have the solution or answer already formed in our minds. Then we blame God when things don't turn out the way we want them to. We have to be honest with ourselves and with God, because He already knows what we want before we ask Him.

- The idea of love will make you do things you would have never dreamed of, like taking him back although he cheats and sleeps with other women; or making excuses for the way he talks to you or even when he has hit you. And in the midst of all the turmoil, I began to see what I had built crumble before me.

- My heart was being torn into pieces because my dream of "happily-ever-after" wasn't coming true. I made choices that did not include God, but I wanted Him to make it okay. I didn't want to face or go through the consequences of my choices, and I wanted God to fix my mess. When the situation was at its worst and my list of fix-it remedies was exhausted, I got on my knees. That is when I needed, wanted, and had to cry out to God like never before for peace and security.

- When I spent alone time with God, He showed me what He wanted was for me to cry out before I got to that place where I needed to cry out to Him. He wants to be a part of my daily activities and life. He wants all of my time, not just the end of my day.

- I learned that no person should ever have the place in your life that is and should be reserved for the Lord. I had placed my heart into the wrong hands. The only One who should ever consume my life like that is Almighty God because the Scripture tells me, "He will keep you in perfect peace when you keep your mind on Him" (Isaiah 26:3, KJV), and I should, "Trust in the Lord with all your heart and lean not unto your own understanding. Acknowledge Him in all your ways, and He will direct your path" (Psalms 3:5-6, NIV).

- I wanted to be loved and in a relationship so badly that I accepted the yokes from each man I was with at the time. But God declared in His Word that there should never be any other gods before Him. But I put all my trust in Robert and how I thought he would treat me and make me feel valued, instead of putting all of my consuming trust in the Lord.

- God's Word should never be used in part to justify personal actions. Instead, be anxious for nothing; wait on God, however long the "wait" is.

PART THREE
MY REFLECTIONS

OWN YOUR STUFF
THAT'S HOW YOU GROW

My journey didn't end there. This was a tragic situation, and there was such loss. I lost my husband. A family lost a son and brother. Robert's three young boys lost their father. My son and daughter now have a distorted image of their mother and live with the fact that I was beaten, raped, and almost killed.

I couldn't help but think about all the people that were affected by my choice to disobey the Word of God. I don't blame myself for Robert's death. He made choices to do the things he did. But, I did take responsibility for my choices and my disobedience to the Word of God.

I knew I'd been torn: torn between religion and relationship. My choices affected more than just me. I needed and wanted to be healed. I knew only One has the power to heal. I didn't want to carry the sadness and hurt of all those I'd affected inside of me like a heavy weight. I didn't want the root of bitterness to take hold in the newly tilled valley of my heart.

When I asked the Lord for forgiveness, I sought answers to the following questions, "How would the mending process start? With whom would it start?"

I learned it could only start with God. It required putting aside my religion and my hope for relationships with men. God was the healthy relationship I was seeking. He is husband of my soul.

CHAPTER NINE

SAYING GOODBYE

Robert's family called me Friday, the day after his death. We discussed the funeral arrangements. They didn't have the money to bury him, so I agreed to pay for his funeral, using the life insurance coverage we had.

Robert's funeral was on Tuesday, July 23, 1996. I decided to go to the funeral home on Monday when no one would be there and I wouldn't have to worry about running into any of his family. Although I agreed to pay for the funeral, I knew I couldn't or should I say "shouldn't" attend the services. Many of his family members blame me for his death, so I didn't want to set myself up for any more drama.

My brother took me to the funeral home to view Robert's body privately and to pay the funeral expenses. John waited in another room as I followed the director into his office. After I had finished signing the paperwork, I asked the director, "What does his body look like?"

He replied, "He was a handsome young man, and we didn't have to do a lot of work." I asked him, "How many times was he shot?"

He answered quietly, "Three times, but we covered the wounds as best we could." He asked if I wanted to view the body, and I said, "Yes."

The funeral director led me to Robert's body, which lay on a table in the hallway. His body was covered with a sheet, but I could see his face. Tears began to well up in me and run down my face. He looked so peaceful. I could see the gunshot wounds that hit him in his face, and

I tried to image the pain he experienced. "Which bullet is the one that killed him?" I wondered. But did it really matter?

I began to sob, and a flood of emotions overcame me. As he lay there, I remember saying, "Why?? It didn't have to end like this. You could have surrendered and still been alive. What made you want to kill me or put yourself in the position to get killed? " It just doesn't make sense. But in retrospect, I guess it did. I immediately remembered what I kept hearing in my spirit, "It's not going to end the way you think."

As I looked at him, I began to think about the fun we had, and even all the arguments. Although I was thankful to be alive, I told him how selfish he had been to put himself in such a position to be killed. He wasn't thinking about his family, his sons, or me.

I wanted to pull the sheet back to look at his body because I was a little confused. The funeral director said he was only shot three times, but when I had gone to the house on Friday there were over twenty markings on the stairwell, on the walls, and in the bedrooms where the bullet holes were. But I was scared of what I might see, and I really didn't want to know or to have that image set in my mind. I just knew his body had bullet wounds because I remember his body jerking from being shot in the vision.

After being there for thirty minutes or so, I leaned over and kissed him. I experienced a sense of closure as I said my "good-byes."

The Day of the Funeral

I woke up on Tuesday morning feeling a little anxious and nervous. I knew Robert's funeral service was going on, and I was trying to imagine how it was going and who would be there. I had talked to Monte's mother, Kathy, the night before, and she told me that she would come by after the funeral to check on me and bring me a copy of Robert's funeral program.

Later that afternoon, Kathy and her sister Tina came by the house. They told me that the service was really sad. They said they would take me to the gravesite so I would know where his body had been laid.

When we got to the cemetery, I got out of the car. I had a hard time walking to the grave. I was overcome with tears and sobbing. The reality had finally set in that my husband was dead, and that I wouldn't have to look over my shoulder and wonder if he was stalking me ever again.

Kathy and Tina were on both sides of me holding me up. They comforted me as I cried and walked me back to the car.

It was over.

CHAPTER TEN

MY RECOVERY

I slept a lot over the next several days. Not only was my body healing, but my mind needed time to heal as well. I realized there was a process to grieving. It would take time to heal physically and mentally.

Each day after the tragedy was hard mentally and emotionally. The pictures of that Thursday night kept vividly running through my mind. I kept reliving each moment. A flood of emotions seemed to overtake me– crying, anger, shame, grief, fear, and feelings of worthlessness. When I least expected it, emotion consumed me.

God's Promise

As I reflected on my journey with Robert, I went back to the beginning of our relationship. God reminded me of His promise and the instructions He gave to me.

> *Robert was not the man He had for me, but if I chose to be with him, I must do three things: learn to trust Him exclusively, study the Word daily to hear His voice, and read I Corinthians 7:10-16. God would keep me through all that was to come.*

I believe my obedience in doing these three things resulted in His fulfilling His promise to me. He did what He said—He kept me. The Lord not only kept me, He kept my family. Not only did God allow Taukia to be released, He saved my brother from harm. Only God knew my brother's mind on the day Robert held me hostage. My brother had resolved in his mind to protect me from Robert. I don't believe John had any way of knowing that Robert would come to my house the same day he was coming to pick up Mom's papers. But God knew the situation, and kept my brother out of harm's way because by the time he got to my neighborhood, the police were on the scene.

While I felt sadness over Robert's putting himself in that situation, I also felt partially responsible. I married a man I knew I shouldn't have. The marital bond is like no other bond or covenant I had experienced. Because of my actions, a part of me died, too. I do not want to imply that he lost his life because of my disobedience, but because of it, the consequences were great, and someone lost. Even in my disobedience, God was my protector and my strength. He worked it out for my good and His glory.

I could have lost my life, but God saw fit to keep me here. He told me, it was not my time.

Knowing Christ is a Journey

Whenever I share my testimony of how the Lord delivered me from the hostage situation, other Christians often ask if I was "Saved" at the time I married Robert. Yes, I tell them. Yes, I knew Christ. I accepted Christ into my heart a long time ago. I was learning and growing spiritually, yet my thinking was still carnal—trying to do things my way.

As I have learned to love myself, accepting me for me, I strive to teach my daughter, who is now a young adult, this same lesson. I went through what I did because I did not love or respect myself. I could not see my worth in my relationships. I did not value myself as God's creation. Though I read the scripture and knew it said I was fearfully and wonderfully made, I did not believe it. However, my insecurities did not begin with the three marriages. I looked back and found the surprising root of my behavior.

In my heart-wrenching, personal search, which exposing many emotions, I found a root that pulled me back to my childhood. Rooted there, in the depths of my heart, was the pain of not feeling accepted as a child. From the time of my youth, I lived feeling like I had to do more to be accepted by others, never realizing I had to accept myself as God's creation first—just the way I am. I had to love myself first, as Christ loves me, before loving someone else.

When I look back, it hurts to know I was so foolish. Even though I graduated at the top of my class from a private school, I had so much to learn. I had book smarts, but I did not know who I was. I was trying to find myself in pleasing everybody else. I was trying to make everybody else comfortable with who I thought I was instead of knowing who I was in Christ.

My validation came from outside—from others who didn't have a clue either. I gravitated to men who I thought would fill the void only God can fill. I just wanted to feel loved. I wanted to be loved by someone other than my parents and family. I yearned to be loved and accepted, to feel that someone valued and wanted me. But in the process, I allowed myself to be used and abused while my heart remained broken, torn and empty. Through this journey, I realized I did not approve of ME. I did not think I was worthy of a "good man." I thought I had to accept whoever came along. But now I know God does not want just anything or anyone for me. He allowed my heart to be torn so I could see that He wanted me to put my heart and trust in Him and not in man. I was meant to be His bride first.

Oh yeah, at the time I married Robert, I thought I was the pillar of strength. I was strong for my children and my family. I was doing it alone (even though I had been married twice before). I thought I was a confident woman. No one could have told me I had low self-esteem. But self-esteem is not based on what you do or how you make things work to survive in life. Self-esteem, or self-love, is the value and worth one has for self. The reality was I found no value in me. I had to be with a man to complete me and make me feel important. I wanted someone to be my "Knight in Shining Armor." He would be my protector—fulfilling my fairy tale.

After the crisis I finally learned it was because I had low self-esteem that I allowed myself to be in situations where a man hit me and cheated on me while I overlooked it and made it my fault. I just turned a deaf ear and a blind eye to what they were doing, and how it was affecting me. I sought validation and love from men who were not capable of giving either. What I needed, they could not give. I needed the Teacher to show me the truth.

This revelation meant releasing some things and some people. I released the hurts and negative emotions I had about my ex-husbands. I released the negative thought, "Having a man (regardless of how he treats you) is better than not having a man at all." I had to erase the old thoughts and ideas and create new ones, images, hopes, and dreams that lined up with the Word of God and His desires for me. As I began to study the Word, Jeremiah 29:11 (NIV) became the foundational scripture I said over and over to myself. "'For I know the plans I have for you,' declares the Lord, 'plans to prosper you and not to harm you, plans to give you hope and a future.'" Although I had read this scripture before, it now was alive in me, and I understood what it meant—that God has a plan for me!

I realize now that the healing process is its own journey. So many questions have to be asked and answered when trying to get to the root of "heart" matters. Questions are the pickax that broke the soil of my heart and allowed the Spirit to find the root in the garden of my heart. Some questions I faced were: What was my relationship with my mother like? What about me and my father? What did those relationships have to do with my marital relationships?

I didn't realize those relationships and how I perceived the roles of my mother and father dictated how I lived and what I looked for in a mate. It had a tremendous effect on my adult life. And, of course, one question often leads to another, making the journey longer and more fluid than expected. However, the journey of self-discovery through Christ's eyes solidified my recovery and ultimately healed my torn heart.

EPILOGUE

The pain experienced during this period of my life was extremely challenging. The Lord stripped away many protective layers that I hid behind in order to keep myself from being hurt. But in the process of creating those protective layers, I was hurting myself because God wanted me to live for Him and to submit myself (mind, body, and soul) totally to Him.

He prepared me for every step of my journey and walked each step with me. I was never alone. God allowed me to go through the experiences because it is part of my purpose and part of His plan.

Part of my purpose is to speak to women about relationships, but how could I speak about something unless I had been through some relationship fire? I couldn't; I wouldn't qualify. I'm now able to speak to women about becoming women of God—that virtuous woman in Proverbs 31. I address topics about relationships, self-esteem, and character building.

It wasn't enough that I had the experiences, but I had to learn from them. I believe the hardest thing is to evaluate one's self and look at the things in your life that are not pleasing to God, or don't line up with what the Word of God says we should do and the way we should live. Being taken hostage forced me to look within.

Yes, I've been married three times. Yes, I was seeking God and have been a member of different churches in search of Him. But what God wanted was a personal relationship with me. It took these experiences in my life for me to realize that and to stop hiding. So my prayer became, "Here I am Lord, change me into only what You want me to be."

As I started developing my new relationship with God, I had to learn to trust again. When I look back, it seems like so many negative things have happened in my life, but it in no way compares to what God is positioning me for, what He is going to do with my experience, and how that experience brought me closer to Him.

My journey gets sweeter as the days go by. I have come to believe God's love for me is unconditional. He validates me. He sends people across my path who confirm His love for me. When I am unsure or when I doubt, He nudges me and reminds me that He's with me.

After I stood over my husband's body, frozen in disbelief, I realized something had to change. I cried out to God daily for strength, for answers, and for the will to make it through tomorrow. My time together with God, through prayer and reading the Word, became more personal. I didn't want to make a step if I didn't think God would be pleased because I've come to realize that obedience to the Word of God is better than the sacrifices we make for the sake of "love." I've learned to wait, not out of fear of making another mistake, but out of knowing I can't make a mistake when God is leading me. In my time with Him, I learned He had a purpose for me, and He loved me enough to give me an assignment—an awesome one. I had to learn to let go of self-pity and guilt and embrace self-love and appreciation. The cycle had to start with me.

My journey could have ended on July 18, 1996, but the Lord wanted me to share my experiences and the love of God with women who are just beginning their own journey in life and with women that are looking for a way out and don't think there is one. My experiences with domestic violence are mild compared to some, and I often wondered, "Why me?"

I know I didn't go through all this just to keep it to myself, but to share it so women can see what God has done in my life and say, "If He did it for her, He'll do it for me." And so the women who are starting in a relationship can say, "I see what she went through, and I don't want to go through anything like that."

When I share my story, women are able to relate to the emotions, thoughts, and feelings that we deal with on a regular basis. And even if you aren't in an unhealthy relationship, you may know someone who is. Domestic violence doesn't see color, age, religion, or sex. Violence in relationships is happening more and more every day. Women and children are dying as a result. I can make a difference now. It is what God, through my journey, has purposed me to do.

PART THREE

APPLICATIONS FROM THE AUTHOR

Learning the Relationship of Unconditional Love

As I look back, I begin to understand why I did the things I did. I marvel at God's unconditional love and that he loves us even when we make bad choices. God will never put on us more than we can handle. But sometimes our choices overshadow His purpose for our lives. We don't always focus on the way God wants us to live, and we often get distracted because we want instant gratification.

Is disobedience worth it? Is the pleasure from sin or disobedience worth losing family, friends, self-worth, or even your life?

No, it shouldn't be and it wasn't worth it for me. But I have learned so much about life and myself; things I really needed to know so I could move forward. These things don't just apply to me, but to everyone who will accept them:

> 1) In our Christian walk, we need to know that life doesn't end when we make negative choices, but our choices will effect something or someone else.
>
> 2) Someone will accept and love you just for you—even if you never change.
>
> 3) God fashioned you in His image, you are lovely and lovable. God does not make mistakes.
>
> 4) If you desire a mate, pray for God to send you a

man fashioned in His image who will treat you like the woman God declares in His Word you are, "fearfully and wonderfully made."

5) God will show you love in its purest form. He always has compassion and shows His unconditional love toward us. His mercies are new every morning.

Don't be afraid to embrace these revelations and acknowledge your insecurities. Lay them at the feet of our heavenly Father in prayer. I guarantee you whenever you're unsure, the Lord has planted seeds from the Word of God which will speak truth to you regarding your self-worth, confidence, acceptance, and assurance. His love covers all our fears.

Celebrate your life, and live knowing that God has a purpose and plan for you. You don't have to figure out what the plan is because He'll show you as you develop a personal relationship with Him by spending time reading the Bible, praying, and talking to Him. He'll always show you the right way to do things.

Wisdom for Stopping the Violence

Women, we can stop domestic violence! You don't have to stay silent! We have to speak up and tell someone that there is a way out. God always gives us a way to escape.

It doesn't matter whether you've ever been in an abusive relationship, or whether you're in one right now. If you're in a relationship, my prayer is that you'll learn something from my experience that will help you make the right choice. Recognize the warning signs beforehand, and make the choice to wait on the relationship God has chosen for you. God's way always turns out better.

When you know who you are and realize you are the best person you will ever know, people will see you in a different light and respect the gifts, talents, and strengths that God has placed in you.

You are "fearfully" and "wonderfully" made!

RESOURCES

It is important to realize there are four categories of abuse: physical, verbal, sexual, and emotional. Please contact The National Domestic Violence Hotline *(http://www.ndvh.org)* for more information on defining domestic violence, preventing it, and escaping from it.

1.800.799.SAFE (7233) 1.800.787.3224 (TTY)
Anonymous & Confidential Help 24/7

Each state and city has resources available. Some in the author's hometown who were helpful to her are listed below with our thanks:

Kansas City, Missouri contact information:
- Battered Women's Hotline & Shelter (816) 861-6100
- Hope House Services for Battered Women (816) 461-4673
- Joyce H. Williams Battered Women's Center (913) 321-0951

ABOUT THE AUTHOR

Janice Butler is a domestic violence survivor who shares her testimony of survival with women and girls. Through difficult times, Janice is learning to be obedient to God and His plan for relationships and marriage. She believes that the Lord allowed her to live through devastating circumstances so can share with others how she has become the victor, rather than remaining a victim. Her vision is to encourage other women to avoid compromise, stand true to the Word of God, and recognize their worth in Christ.

Janice is a speaker and founder of *Woman of Character Ministry* in Kansas City, Missouri. She raised two children, a son and a daughter, as a single mother.